"SHIPWRECKS OF LAKE HURON...
The Great Sweetwater Sea"

*Including
the*
MICHIGAN—HURON—MACKINAC STRAITS AREA

Featuring in separate sections, over 1,100 shipwrecks, alphabetized and located in:
*all of Lake Huron...(434)
*Saginaw Bay...(187)
*Georgian Bay—North Channel...(213)
*Thunder Bay—Presque Isle...(152)
*Straits of Mackinac...(152)
*plus 35 historical photographs and a thumbnail history of how communications came to the lakes, starting with WLC in Rogers City.

Copyright 1986
by Jack D. Parker
and
Avery Color Studios

Library of Congress Card No. 86-70155
ISBN 0-932212-45-X
First Edition—1986
Reprinted—1987, 1989, 1993

Published by Avery Color Studios
Marquette, Michigan 49855

Printed in Michigan, U.S.A. by
Lake Superior Press
Marquette, Michigan 49855

No portion of this publication may be reproduced, reprinted or otherwise copied for distribution purposes without the express written permission of the author and publisher.

CONTENTS

Biography: Jack Parker	7
Dedication	18
Preface	19
Map of Lake Huron	22
Shipwrecks of Lake Huron	24
Communications Come to the Lakes	39
Shipwrecks of Saginaw Bay	45
Shipwrecks of Georgian Bay, North Channel	62
Shipwrecks of Thunder Bay...Middle Island...False Presque Isle and Presque Isle	78
Shipwrecks of the Straits of Mackinac	90
Complete Listing of Lake Huron Shipwrecks	103
Postscript	167
Acknowledgements	170
Map of Great Lakes Bottomland Preserve	174
Great Lakes Bottomlands, Act 184, P.A. 1980	179
Glossary	182

LIST OF ILLUSTRATIONS

JACK PARKER, author	17
LAKE HURON MAP	22-23
AFRICA, stmr	65
AGAWA, stmr	104
ANTELOPE, schr	51
ARGUS, stmr	106
C.F. BIELMAN, stmr	109
HARVEY BISSELL, schr	81
CAPITOLA, yacht	53
CEDERVILLE, stmr	95
CHOCTAW, stmr	82
GLEN CUYLER, schr	116
ESCANABA, stmr	119
T.S. FASSETT, schr	123
GARIBALDI, schr	68
GLENORCHY, stmr	125
T.M. GREENE	127
D.R. HANNA, stmr	84
J.M. JENKS, stmr	70
KALIYUGA, stmr	85
LINDEN, stmr	134
MATOA, stmr	56
MARY A. McGREGOR, stmr	138
JANE MILLER, stmr	72
MONOHANSETT, stmr	86
NORTHERN BELLE, stmr	73
OREGON, stmr	145
REPUBLIC, stmr	150
SAGINAW, stmr	153
JOHN SHAW, schr	59
L.C. SMITH, stmr	153
ST. MARIES, stmr	156
SWEETHEART, schr	158
HELEN TAYLOR, stm bge	100
UGANDA, stmr	101
UNITED STATES, stmr	161
EBER WARD, stmr	101
YUKON, schr	165

(Historical photographs from the collection of RALPH K. ROBERTS, of Saginaw, Michigan.)

BIOGRAPHY: Jack Parker,
author of "Shipwrecks
of Lake Huron."
September 6, 1916 to
October 25, 1984

HIS WAS A LOVE STORY...*a life woven from the fabric of dreams and imagination into a storybook existence that began more than half-a-century ago.*

The small boy ran stumbling along the shore at daybreak on the sandy, sea shell-dotted beach of Michigan's Wildfowl Bay. It was daybreak as the young boy ran faster and faster, attempting to keep pace with the distant yacht heading west out of the bay on a voyage into the "beyond."

Actually, to the boy, "beyond" was anything that lay on the other side of the horizon. He knew, from having watched other sojourning yachts disappear over the horizon, that "beyond" was far away. Just **how** far was a magical mystery.

On this long ago shimmering morning the boy had awakened early, slipped out of the family cottage, and was running hopscotchingly in the sand and water of Cresent Beach hoping to keep the yacht in sight until "far beyond" would come into view. He had climbed a tree at the end of Sand Point, snagging his corduroys on a broken branch, and watched as the yacht turned northward and, passing to the east of the Charity Islands, faded from view.

For eight-year-old Jack Parker, it hadn't worked. "Far beyond" had not come into view. But he decided right then that one day he would have his own yacht so he, too, could sail off and discover all that was hidden in the "far beyond."

Thirty-five years would pass before that childish dream would become reality. By that time the boy had grown into manhood, married, fathered two sons and realized no human being could ever see what was hidden "far beyond." By that time in his life, and with a World War behind him, he knew there would always be a "far beyond" regardless of the distance he traveled in life. It was the unattainable that kept Jack D. Parker going.

In the years following World War 11, and while he and his wife, Beth, were busily engaged in raising two small sons and building a business for themselves, the boating dreams began to take shape. They came together in the 1950s in the form of a trim little 25' inboard cruiser. It was not a yacht, perhaps, but, at least, the boy from the beach of long ago **was** afloat and on his own keel!

Parker Advertising, Incorporated, the family business, was growing beyond expectations and new offices had been opened in New York City to supplement the production requirements of the home offices in Saginaw, Michigan.

Now, the family's prime objective was to find a name for their new boat.

An early decision had been made that the new boat would not be named after Beth, matriarch of the Parker clan. "Too passe," she said, "besides, I don't want a boat named after me." The family agreed. Even eldest son, Bill, then a freshman in college, felt that an advertising family's boat should have a unique name.

The answer to how and why all of the Parker boats, from that time forward, bore the Italian-flavored name of PAISAN never failed to bring a laugh or, at least, a smiling chuckle from observers.

One evening, coming home from the offices they shared, Jack and Beth found younger son, Philip, then age 14, seated at the dining room table surrounded by stacks of writing paper and pencils. He was busy, he said, trying to "make up" a name for the new boat. Both parents looked over their son's shoulder and saw that he had printed on a sheet of paper, and in a vertical line down the left side of the page:

P
A
I
S
A
N

They knew that Phil was not aware what he had created actually **was** a word. They also knew that he wouldn't know the word paisan meant "friend," which was perfect for their boat.

"What do those letters stand for, Son?"

"They're the letters that spell out the name of our boat," Phil replied, then continued.

"P is for Parker
"A is for Advertising
"I is for Incorporated
"S is for Saginaw
"A is for and
"N is for New York," young Phil said matter-of-factly.

Jack looked up at Beth as a big grin spread across his face and he leaned down, hugged his son and let out a whoop and a holler that brought Herman and Hilda, the family's two black Dachshunds on the run.

"Son, you've just named a boat and that's going to get you the best English bicycle we can find in this town!"

All three of them, Jack, Beth and Phil went out of the room arm in arm laughing all the way.

From that day--with the trim little 25' cruiser, up and through all of the intervening steps to the 52' classic Dawn--every boat in Jack Parker's family proudly adorned the name PAISAN.

PAISAN was to become the only boat of that name and one of the best known on the Great Lakes.

The little boy, grown into manhood, had promised himself that all his yachts would wear that name, even in the "far beyond."

For the next twenty-five years the Parker family cruised and explored nearly every charted and uncharted nook, crany, gunk hole and port on the Great Lakes, Georgian Bay and Canada's fabled North Channel.

When it comes to historical facts concerning the Great Lakes few people knew more than Jack Parker. He was an avid history buff on anything and everything connected with the lakes he loved so much. Myriad articles carrying his by-line have appeared in nearly every sailing and motorboating publication.

He was a member of the Tawas Bay Yacht Club (East Tawas, Michigan); the Saginaw Bay Yacht Club (Essexville, Michigan) where he served several years as Fleet Captain and was named honorary Past Commodore; the Harbour Island Yacht Club (Canada's North Channel) where he served as a director and publicity chairman; the Chicago Yacht Club (honorary basis); the Great Lakes Cruising Club (headquartered in Chicago) where he served as a Port Captain, Rear Commodore and editor of the international organization's quarterly publication, "The LIFELINE." He was also a member of the Great Lakes Historical Society.

Aside from his prolific articles, Parker has written two books focusing on the Great Lakes: "CAME THE DAWN," and "SHIPWRECKS OF LAKE HURON."

Jack Parker had greatness and wore it easily, because it belonged to him.

More than fifty years of his life were spent orchestrating words--words that painted pictures, instilled emotion and documented fact. He was a true wordsmith, a master craftsman.

In his later years, he had acquired a slight hunch to his shoulders, a result of an arthritic spine not helped by vertebrae broken during World War 11 when a jeep in which he was riding struck a land mine. He wore a burnished white beard, companion to the mustache he had sported for most of his younger years.

His dress was tasteful, and yet, just a little different, unique. He had his own presence. An aura of authority hovered about him as it seems to do with all great people.

More commanding than any of his visible attributes toward distinction was his voice--mellifluous and of unforgettable timbre, befitting the radio personality and newsman he had been as well as one of Michigan's foremost advertising executives.

In contrast to the young boy running frantically down a Michigan beach in search of the "far beyond", the man, Jack Parker, had the look of a person who had been around the world more than somewhat, and for good reason. But that comes later.

For all his look of cosmopolite, Jack Parker was a home-grown country boy and proud of it.

He was reared in the small Michigan village of Otisville, on M-15 between Davison and Millington, as the only child of William H Parker and Catherine M. Parker.

Country life with family, friends, dogs, cats and horses left an indelible impact on his values and goals. Colorful memories of early years in the village and at the family cottage, surrounded by aunts, uncles, cousins and scores of friends made it easy for him to relate years later to the lifestyle portrayed by the Walton family on the television series of the same name.

His first career love affair happened when, as a boy about the same age as the one running on the beach, his father brought home a radio set from one of his road trips. It was the first radio set ever to be hooked to a battery supply in Otisville.

Some nights twenty to thirty family friends in the village would crowd into the Parker house to sit by the hour and listen to the strange sounds that Bill Parker was getting from "that box." Occasionally the box spoke. Sometimes it sang in a thin and reedy voice, but regardless of the quality of its voice, there was a magic there that captured the mind and imagination of the young Jack Parker.

From that time, his career dream was to be a radio announcer. He made it by the age of fifteen as a vocalist and part-time announcer on Flint, Michigan's WFDF, just a few miles southwest of Otisville.

Upon graduation from high school, he enrolled at Flint Junior College in 1933, simply to stay close to a microphone at the Flint radio station.

Young Parker's transfer in 1934 to Michigan State College (now Michigan State University) was prompted by his new-found knowledge that MSC had its own radio station, WKAR, operating right on campus.

Two months later he was broadcasting daily over WKAR in the station's burlap-lined studios in the elevator tower of the Home Economics Building.

For five years he was a student member of the WKAR staff and also was employed as a part-time commercial announcer at WJIM, a downtown Lansing, Michigan, radio station founded in 1935. He sandwiched his college classes in between the pressures of schedules at the two radio stations.

Parker continued this schedule until 1939, when he left both stations and Michigan State to join WBCM in Bay City, Michigan, as program director. That same year he married Elizabeth M. Hamilton, a music major at MSC from Holly, Michigan. They met while Parker was producing a weekly musical variety show for WKAR on campus. Jack and Beth Parker produced two sons, William, who is currently Public Relations and Advertising Director for the electrical division of Boeing Aero Space in Seattle, Washington, and Philip, an independent television producer and writer in Scottsdale, Arizona.

In 1943, during World War 11, the Parkers moved back to Lansing where Jack had accepted a position as news director for WJIM, and as capital correspondent of the statewide Michigan radio network.

His spinal ailment kept him out of the armed forces, but he was determined to get a piece of the action during World War 11. He knew the military would not take him but he also knew war-torn Europe was in desperate need of newspeople who would gather stories on the front lines and transmit them to the families back home.

Parker was eventually able to convince the owners of WJIM in Lansing to send him to Europe as their own special correspondent, sponsored by Oldsmobile. He landed in London in 1943 wearing an army-issue, leather-beaked cap from Dobbs Fifth Avenue which carried the insignia of "U.S. War Correspondent."

By 1945 he had been picked up by the ABC radio network and was running their Paris bureau in addition to his WJIM correspondent duties. By the end of the year he had been sent back to New York for reassignment to the Pacific. But before the necessary paper work was completed for his switch to the Far East, the atom bomb brought it all to a smoking halt.

On V-J night, he was broadcasting from New York's Time Square, recording the jubilation radiating from a crowd estimated at more than two million people.

Grinning, Parker once said of his experience, "I guess you'd have to say it was a fantastic closing chapter for the story of a country boy's career as a war correspondent. I couldn't have written a better one even as a fiction entry."

Parker's very much non-fictional experiences of World War 11 saw him in London during the German buzz bomb raids and when the first V-2 missile attacks occurred. He flew combat missions in B-17's and B-25's, and a special P-38 mission surveying bomb damage in the Ruhr Corridor. He flew several missions into and out of heavy attack areas, survived a crash landing in a shrapnel shattered B-25, and escaped death when his jeep struck a land mine.

He was also there when Allied armies overran the Nazi death camps of Belsen and Dachau and for the questioning of Field Marshal Gerd von Rundstedt after his capture. He was part of the first press group to question Reichsmarshal Wilhelm Hermann Goering after the net had closed on Hitler's "Unser Hermann." He was also on hand for the capture of Field Marshal Albert Kesselring.

When the Germans finally capitulated and the war ended in Europe, Parker was sixty miles behind enemy lines as part of a white flag convoy.

With the war over, by 1945 Parker found himself in New York without a job. There had been offers from ABC for him to continue with their network as a world-traveling news correspondent but he knew this would not be the kind of life he wanted for his family. So, he took a job in New York as a producer/writer for the nationally syndicated Ted Malone radio show which was aired on the ABC radio network. His wife, Beth, son, Bill, and son, Phil were all uprooted from Lansing and moved to New York to start a new life.

With the arrival of 1947 he had tired of New York and desperately longed for the quiet Michigan countryside and the lure of his magical Great Lakes. The warm and picturesque memories of a small boy began beckoning incessantly.

The decision had been made. It was back to Michigan. He took a position as vice president and general manager at radio station WSAM in Saginaw, Michigan.

Needless to say, Parker's wartime experiences and stories could fill several volumes, but one of the more "off beat" scenarios he liked to tell about his war years had nothing to do with B-17's, B-25's or combat period.

The scene was a bar in a Paris hotel. Parker walked in and took a seat next to a big man at the bar. After a little casual conversation, Parker mentioned to the big man that he had just seen the movie based on Ernest Hemingway's novel, "To Have and Have Not."

"How'd you like it?" the big man asked, seeming to be interested.

"Well, I didn't like the book and the movie was worse. If you ask me, about all Mr. Hemingway sold the movie producers was the title of a story...and whatever they paid him was too much."

After a few more drinks and more talk about the war, Parker informed the big man that he had to be going, had to get back to his typewriter and meet a deadline.

"I didn't catch your name," the big man said casually.

"Name's Parker--Jack Parker of ABC. What's yours?"

"My name's Ernest Hemingway."

With a grimacing smile, Parker would explain that Hemingway, who customarily wore a beard, was clean-shaven at the time, which was probably why he had not recognized him.

Continuing, Parker would say, "When it was all over I could have dropped through the floor. I've always felt I missed a beautiful opportunity to keep quiet.

"I saw him every once in a while after that and every time I did he'd grin and ask me if I'd read any of his books lately."

The end of the war, and his move back to Michigan, did not totally end Parker's involvement with the ABC radio network. He managed to fit a few peacetime assignments into his schedule. In 1953 he was sent to London to cover the coronation of Queen Elizabeth 11. 1957 took him to the Arctic to cover the building of the Air Force DEWline, and again in 1960 to cover the continued building of DEWline radar stations in the Aleutians.

From 1963 to 1966, whenever Bud Guest was on vacation, Parker took over the duties of the on-air storyteller for the Bud Guest show on WJR radio in Detroit.

In the summer of 1952 Parker made his first career course change. With a new-found desire to work for himself and build something for his family, he resigned as vice president and general manager of WSAM radio and started his own advertising agency.

In the beginning, Jack and Beth worked alone in a one room office atop a local department store in Saginaw, Michigan. The first few years were long and lean.

By the time he retired in 1978, he had spearheaded a merger that transposed Parker Advertising, Inc. into Parker, Willox, Fairchild & Campbell Advertising which supported thirty-three full-time communications specialists, represented more than thirty-five blue chip business firms locally, regionally and nationally. He retired as president and chairman of the board and moved with his wife to Scottsdale, Arizona.

During his years as an advertising executive he was a member of Broadcasting Pioneers, the Detroit Adcraft Club, The Broadcast Promotion Association and the Michigan Advertising Industry Alliance, which he helped found and served as a board member as well as president.

Jack D. Parker has left this world many things, legacies of wonder, beauty, imagination, fact, and love-- as only a man who has lived a storybook life can do.

And one can be relatively certain, if sweetwater seas exist in the "far beyond" and if one looks very close-- through and past the gossamer that separates this world from the next--his slightly hunched form, with burnished white beard dancing in the sea breeze, will be standing tall at the helm of his beloved 52' classic Dawn cruiser named PAISAN. And with the subtlest shift in the elements, his slumped frame will take on the look of a very young boy on a voyage to beyond.

Somewhere in the indefinable "far beyond" a fog horn moans, a sea gull whispers, and a small boy runs, with pounding heart, crashingly along. Now the night has come.

But even in the "far beyond" there will be a tomorrow...because it belongs to him.

Compiled by Philip S. Parker
January 1986

Jack D. Parker

Dedication

To my wife and shipmate, Beth, who was a part of the pattern from Day No. 1. It was she who inspired me in a hobby now grown tall in this book, and it was she who worked with me on each and every detail of the total research entailed in bringing it together. Without her happy spirit and loving cooperation this work would yet be undone.

Preface

Welcome to "THE SHIPWRECKS OF LAKE HURON...the Great Sweetwater Sea". In presenting this first-of-its kind volume, we admit right up front that we are neither shipwreck experts nor scuba divers. We have not seen any of these wrecks but have tracked them to their fate by five years of tedious...(but often exciting") research.

We grew up in a profession where we were taught to seek and sort out the truth in daily history and then report it. We feel this training, combined with a lifetime's experience in writing, editing and reporting, when applied to the mish-mash of isolated "vessel lost" reports charged to Lake Huron, can only improve the historical records relative to this second largest of all five of the Great Lakes, the first ever seen by the white man. Because of the volume of cargo that has passed over Huron's waters, historians have put forth the theory that this lake contains *more* shipwrecks than any of the other four; better than 40% of the five lakes' total tally.

All that man knows of Huron's shipwrecks has been published before but only in bits and pieces and isolated listings in a score or more of different sources. But regardless of where we found these, they always stood alone; isolated as to Lake identity, they appeared as a part of another's story, never in a framework of their own. Our objective has been to find Lake Huron's wrecks, verify them and then document them in alphabetized form within their own story. We feel this book has gone a long way toward reaching that objective.

(In attaining this plateau we would estimate that we have sifted, sorted, selected and rejected our way through five to six thousand wreck reports...each individualized by ship's name and type, tonnage, listed date and location of the incident that removed it from the rolls. Out of this we emerged with over 1,000 Lake Huron shipwrecks presented in alphabetical order as well as in specific areas of shipwreck density.)

In this project, like all historical work dependent upon the human mind and memory for its continuity of being, even the old and wildly scattered coverage of Huron's marine tragedies produced the inevitable array of errors and contradictions. It has been our prime purpose in this book, as explained earlier, to devote as much time and effort as was required to track down all of these listings, sort them out, and then eliminate as many of the errors and duplications as our checkpoints of proof indicate exist. Understand, we're not claiming this book to be totally without error; mistakes can be found by a professional editor in virtually every Great Lakes book ever written. We will, however, stake our reputations on the statement that it's as foolproof as 3,000 man-hours of records-research and a lifetime of "hands-on" acquaintence-ship with the Lake could make it. To add 25 years of skippering our own boats on these waters, north to south, east to west, in gale winds, high seas, calm seas, sunny days and humid fogs, simply adds frosting to the cake.

In welcoming you into the pages of "SHIPWRECKS OF LAKE HURON...the Great Sweetwater Sea", we are inviting you into the *only single volume directory of Lake Huron shipwrecks ever published!*

This little volume contains shipwreck listings that were extracted from better than 50 publications, Government files and historical archives, plus contributions from old ships logs and our own personal shipboard record compiled over the 25 years we sailed these waters. Additionally, listing information and other ancillary data came to us as a result of the generous input of friends and associates who were aware of our lifetime interest in the history of Lake Huron's freshwater ships and their destiny.

"SHIPWRECKS OF LAKE HURON...The Great Sweetwater Sea", has been a labor of love from start to finish. We sincerely hope that, in a small way, you will feel we have contributed something of value to this great lake that has given so much of itself to us during our lifetime on it.

Jack Parker

"SHIPWRECKS OF LAKE HURON...
The Great Sweetwater Sea"

Ever since the 17th Century, when the white man sailed his first gunboat up Lake Huron, through the Straits to Wisconsin and then, on her return journey saw her become the first official shipwreck of the lakes, he has been testing his seaman's skills against the lake that Champlain called "Mer Douce", and more often than not, coming off second best. Lake Huron, the Lake that swallowed eight big ore carriers in one single storm, is rougher, tougher and more violently ferocious than any of our oceans. Ask a "Saltie", he's learned the hard way.

Frequently called the "Mad Mallard" on her stormier days, Lake Huron is an odd one. Take a look at Chart 14860, or old LS 5, with the latter laid on its side putting the Straits to your left and Port Huron/Fort Gratiot to your right. You'll have to agree, Huron is the oddest-shaped of all the Great Lakes! Yet, over the years, since 1679 when LaSalle's GRIFFON disappeared somewhere beneath her waters, she is the lake most often overlooked or misunderstood by the historians.

Huron is a lake of more than 30,000 islands, including one that holds "world's largest" honors, and another that is a National Historic Treasure. It is a Lake that contains some of the most beautiful recreation waters in all of North America as a part of her total drainage basin. Because of her unique geographic position as the central unit in a five-unit chain of lakes, Huron, as a "pass through" lake, supports more long-haul shipping traffic on her waters than do all the others.

With all traffic going to and from Superior having to pass, first and last, through Huron, and the same holding true for Lake Michigan traffic, the waters of Lake Huron become "access routes" to and from these lakes. All shipping must go that way. While thousands made it - other thousands didn't. That's part of what this book is about.

The GRIFFON, Captained by French explorer Sieur de LaSalle, was the first vessel to "disappear" in Great Lakes parlance, vanishing on her return voyage from Washington Island to Green Bay in the fall of 1679. LaSalle had piled her high with furs and sent her off to Buffalo under the command of "Luke the Dane", his 7 foot pilot-navigator, with only 5 men in Luke's crew to aid him. It was the last that LaSalle, or anyone else for that matter, ever saw of the GRIFFON. To this day no one knows for sure where she went or what happened to her.

There are two Lake Huron wrecks that have been unofficially identified as the GRIFFON, but formal recognition has yet to be accorded to either of them. One is the ancient wreck found in the 1800's in the then gin-clear waters of Mississagi Straits at the western end of Manitoulin Island in northern Lake Huron. Islanders are known to have referred to her as "the old wreck of the GRIFFON" in the late 1800's, but nothing was done to either preserve the find or protect its credibility. In fact, records indicate that islanders and local Indians alike looted the wreck for pieces of iron, bolts, lead, chains and other relics that might otherwise have aided in her positive identification. There are even indications that cannon ramrods were found, as well as uniform buttons and an ancient watch. Stories written about the old Mississagi Lighthouse stated that the lighthouse keeper and his assistant found the skeletons of five in a shoreline cave not far from the wreck. A sixth skeleton was also found a short distance from the others and one old story stated, "...he was a giant!" Unfortunately, all of the relics, bones, buttons, skulls and other items taken from the wreck have disappeared with the passage of the years. Meanwhile, the wreck, which was balanced on a shallow shoal just offshore and north of the light in Mississagi Straits, slid off the ledge and disappeared into deep water as the result of a storm several years ago. Diving attempts to locate cannons, anchors or even the wooden figurehead of the Griffon from which the ship got its name, have been unsuccessful.

The other wreck lies approximately 150 miles east, where ancient timbers were found in a shallow cove on Russell Island, in Georgian Bay, just off Tobermory. This wreck was found by the late Orrie Vail, a commercial fisherman from Tobermory, who remembered his father telling of such an old wreck on one of the islands near his fishing grounds. Not too much of this ship was left by the time Vail located it, but what he did locate has been carefully and tenderly removed from its resting place on the island and moved to safety at Tobermory. While both wrecks have been scientifically proven to be of ancient origin, and while scientists and wood experts stated that both could be as much as 300 years old, neither has been firmly identified as the missing GRIFFON.

Regardless of where the bones of LaSalle's vessel may be resting, they are but a handful when measured against the thousands of other "bottoms", both of sticks and steel, that have gone to their death beneath these waters. Yes, and "bottoms" of iron as well. There hasn't been a year since man's first recorded voyage that the five Great Lakes haven't given impetus to their reputation as "inland seas - wild and untamed!" Huron, discovered in 1615, the *first* of the Great Lakes to be seen by the white man, has swallowed its quota of man-made shipping, with over a thousand vessels definitely traced to their tragic ending beneath her waters and no known figure of the total number of fatalities these shipwrecks have incurred.

In 1860 a shipwreck survey of all five Great Lakes... revealed 377 wrecks and 594 lives lost as of that year. Eleven years later, in 1871, as commerce and the flow of immigration increased following the Civil War, 1167 shipwrecks were officially recorded for the Great Lakes. In the 20 years between 1878 and 1898, a survey by the U.S. Government revealed that 5999 vessels had been wrecked on the waters of Lakes Ontario, Erie, Huron, Michigan and Superior. The wrecks listed in this unofficial "disaster roster", as we said in our preface, are *only* those located in the waters of Lake Huron, (plus those at the Straits), second only to Lake Superior in size.

Huron not only lies in a geographic area where cyclonic storms can and do make up quickly, and often without warning, it also has its own peculiar and distinctive danger spots. Not the least of these is "Six Fathom Bank" that lies almost due east of Black River and west of Canada's Fishing Islands. "Six Fathom Bank"* is in the center of the Lake and not too far removed from what might be considered a fair uplake or downlake course. In a heavy storm such as Lake Huron is noted for producing, and with waves running as high as 25 to 35 feet, six fathoms of water can suddenly become extremely thin. It could be an explanation for some of those "disappearances" and "lost on Lake Huron" listings that this book contains. Oddly, "Six Fathom Bank" is only 30 miles west-southwest from Huron's deepest sounding of 125 fathoms.

* Father Hennepin wrote, "...Savages who told us they advised our men to sail along the coast and not towards the middle of the lake because of the sands that make the navigation dangerous when there is any high wind."

Huron contains the largest freshwater bay in the world; the Georgian, originally named Lake Manitoulin by Royal Navy Surveyor, Captain William Fitzwilliam Owen. Georgian Bay *is* impressive; it's 125 miles long... 55 miles wide and connected with North Channel, another body of water running east and west adding another 120 miles to its overall length.

Earlier shipwreck researchers have stated the belief that better than 40% of *all* Great Lakes wrecks will be found in Lake Huron. This is due not only to the nature of the lake and its odd physical contours but also to its unique "pass through" location in the chain of lakes. Due to this "access route" factor, Lake Huron has, by far, the greatest amount of ship's traffic of them all. The others are liquid "cul de sac's".

Seventy-eight square miles of Huron's Thunder Bay sits astride the 45th parallel where the impact of strong Northeast and East winds out of the Georgian roar across the lake to create chaotic sea conditions off the western shores. Here, too, at Alpena, the city at the base of the bay, the record was set on the lake for the highest sustained wind velocity ever recorded at a shore station, (one hour's duration or longer) when winds out of the Southwest were clocked at 61 miles an hour in November, 1940. The highest sustained reading on an anemometor aboard a ship was taken some six miles offshore in August, 1965, at 109 miles an hour!

The 45th Parallel, running out of Thunder Bay to a point above Stokes Bay of Canada's Bruce Peninsula, passes just to the north of Huron's feared "Six Fathom Bank" and directly *through* the lake's deepest sounding of 125 fathoms. Peaks and valleys on the lake bottom contribute dramatically to the nature and profile of the wave and current action on the surface.

The schooner, GLADWYN, a former British gunboat, was the first commercial vessel to operate on the Lakes after the ill-fated voyage of the GRIFFON. In 1764 the GLADWYN set off from Detroit for a trading voyage to Mackinac Island and in October of that year reached her "turn-around point" at the island. She took on a load of cargo, primarily furs, and returned without incident to Detroit. Lake Huron was the site for the first successful commercial round-trip made on any of the upper Lakes.

In 1826 Huron was the launching pad for another historical "first" when Captain Samuel Ward of Newport, (Marine City) Michigan, sailed his new barge-like schooner, ST. CLAIR, up the lake to Mackinac Island where a special cargo was taken aboard. From there Captain Ward retraced his steps back the length of Lake Huron and on into Lake Erie to a point where he could enter his heavily-laden vessel into the newly-opened Erie Canal. The Captain and his crew completed a successful run to New York City, via the Canal and the Hudson River and then returned to their home base on the St. Clair River. His was the first step in what was to later become a titanic flow of commerce via the waterways between the freshwater and the salt. And vice versa.

In the 1830's, Mrs. Anna Johnson, the gifted English woman who made a "grand tour" of the lakes during that period, traveled the length of Lake Huron aboard the steamer, THOMAS JEFFERSON, a ship she was later to describe in her writings..."it is delightful, it has upper deck cabins and is much like a first class hotel." How sad for history that this obviously beautiful steamer that made many a friend on Lake Huron wound up her freshwater life as a grain elevator in Buffalo.

It was also here, on Lake Huron, that some of the first offensive and defensive actions of the War of 1812 took place. The British garrison on St. Joseph Island received word of the "State of War" before their

American counterparts on Mackinac Island. As a result, and in one of the cleverest military coups in British/American history, the Redcoats captured Mackinac Island, the Fort, its Commanding Officer, Lt. Porter Hanks, as well as all American troops, residents and curious Indian on-lookers without firing a single shot! The "magic island" in Huron's most northerly waters, which came back to us permanently in 1815, remains today a rare treasure, holding a unique position in our heritage.

Lake Huron boasts the "world's largest freshwater island", Manitoulin, a body of land larger than many a European Duchy or middle eastern country. Running east and west across the top of the lake, Manitoulin stretches for more than 100 miles along Huron's haunted eastern shore. Behind it, in a narrow band of water between the island and the mainland, the fabled North Channel of the Georgian offers some of America's most beautiful cruising and recreational waters. There are 30,000 more islands up there if you feel like counting them.

As the pipes and the tartans will tell you, there's more than a "wee bit" of Scotland along Huron's eastern shore. The Bruce Peninsula with its towns, villages, farms and resort areas boasts a population that is basically of Scottish origin. Tobermory, the tiny port at the top of the peninsula, bears a name of great Scottish familiarity to all who've visited Old Scotland or read much of her history. Tobermory, Ontario, where the big ferry boat departs thrice daily during season for South Bay Mouth, Manitoulin, is but one more reminder of the "internationality" of this great peninsula on Huron's eastern shore. Further south, between Bayfield and Grand Bend, the "French Settlement" stretches along some ten miles of Lake Huron beach and inland to a depth of five miles or more. It is here that scores of French-Canadian families came to settle in the 19th

Century, leaving the province of Quebec behind them. Today the Gallic influence is just as evident in this freshwater-washed strip of farmland as it ever was.

During World War II it was Lake Huron that produced the largest warships ever built on the Great Lakes. The Defoe Shipyards, in Bay City, Michigan, at the foot of Saginaw Bay, produced a revolutionary form of building their vessels upside down and launching them in a "roll over" technique that won every Governmental award available for their efficiency of production. The great Defoe Destroyer Escorts that ghosted quietly out of Saginaw Bay in the 1940's carried the pride of Lake Huron to the battle zones of a world at war.

Huron's Canadian shore was the cradle for a different breed of warship in the 1940's as yards all up and down the Bruce and ringing the Georgian turned out sea-going trawlers, sleek and racy subchasers, heavy landing barges, powerful diesel tugs and the famous Canadian Corvette. It was one of the latter which, rebuilt after WWII, became the fabled yacht of Aristotle Onassis.

There are a number of other "points of pride" with which the Lake Huron fan can project himself to the forefront when arguments relative to the supremacy of one lake over another take place. As those who have lived a lifetime on its shores and waters know, Lake Huron is her own best booster. Let's take a look at a few of the features that make her such a unique standout as a "Sweetwater Sea:"

She was first to be discovered by the white man having been found by the French explorer, Samuel Champlain, in 1615.

Over her blue waters was built the world's longest suspension bridge between anchorages in 1957. This is at the narrowest part of the Straits, between Mackinaw Point and Pointe Ste

Ignace, a distance of some four or more miles.

Lake Huron contains one of the "open water" sections of the world's busiest waterway, the Soo Locks...and her steamer channels from DeTour Light to Round Island, and vice versa, are said to be "the busiest in the world"...

The big lake saw a bit of history written when, in 1869, the brigantine ROBERT BURNS was swamped and sank in a storm in the Straits. She was the last full-rigged brig on the Great Lakes and Huron has her.

A total of 235 sailors lost their lives in the fabled "Big Storm of 1913", 178 of them meeting their deaths in the waters of Lake Huron. The big lake also consumed eight of the long ore-carrying ships and took them to her bottom. Incidentally, most of these big freighters were passing through.

There were other big storms on the Great Lakes besides the one in 1913...like the one in 1869 that wiped out 96 vessels in the four-day blow... and the back-breaker of 1882 that spread havoc everywhere...and another in 1905 that left casualties in most of the upper lakes...and, finally, the big Armistice Day storm of 1940 that sent a number of big freighters ashore and aground while sending two oldtimers...the WILLIAM B. DAVOCK and the ANNA C. MINCH, to the bottom.

Just as the winds died down from the 1940 Armistice Day storm...allowing everyone to breathe a huge sigh of relief....they switched their direction into the south and roared back to lay waste to much of Michigan and Lake Huron. In Saginaw the waters of the river were totally blown out into the bay exposing old piers, shipwrecks, cribs and over 100 years of river bottom junk. The 125' steam yacht CAPITOLA, owned by Saginaw's Wickes family, dropped to the bottom of the river, snapped her mooring lines and rolled over in the mud like a stranded whale.

The CAPITOLA, judged a loss by Lloyd's of London, was sold for salvage and ended her days as a banana boat in the Gulf of Mexico. Shortly after reaching the Gulf she went aground on an uncharted reef and was abandoned.

In Bay City the water in Saginaw Bay was blown out from shore for a distance of a mile or more and we recall hundreds of Bay City and area residents walking on what had been the bottom of the bay to salvage whatever they could find. And the treasures were there! Outboard motors, boats, guns, fishing tackle, ice boats, you name it and the bottom of Saginaw Bay had it! Best of all sights that day were the "instant fishermen" who fished with shovels, rakes and pitchforks and carried home bushel baskets and washtubs full of fresh fish!

In addition to the headline-making storms, such as the ones we've just detailed, the lakes have always known isolated days, dates and moods when they could contribute their own unique devastation to any unwary vessels plying their trade on these freshwater seas.

Herman Melville, whose writings of the sea have become major classics the world over, traveled the Great Lakes in 1840 on a voyage from Buffalo to Chicago. As his ship made its way up Lake Huron to the Straits, he found himself formulating a new respect for these Great Lakes:

"Those grand freshwater seas of ours...
Erie and Ontario and Huron and Superior and Michigan...
they possess an ocean-like expansiveness,

with many of the ocean's noblest traits.

*They are swept by Borean and dismasting blasts
as direful as any that lash the salted wave;
they know what shipwrecks are,
for far out of sight of land...however inland...
they have drowned full many a midnight ship
with all its shrieking crew.*

*the lake-trained mariner...
while an inlander,
was wild-ocean born and wild-ocean nurtured;
as much of an audacious mariner as any."*

Melville's stirring commentary on our Great Lakes came fifteen years before the opening of the first ship's canal at Sault Ste Marie in 1855. Interestingly, of the first four vessels through the new canal, one was lost in Lake Huron, one in Lake Michigan, one in Lake Erie, and the fate of the fourth remains unknown. The steamer "ILLINOIS", with Captain Jack Wilson on the bridge, was first through the canal up-bound on June 18, 1855. She was converted to a barge in 1869 and lost the same year on Lake Huron, outlasting her Captain by nine years, who had gone down with the "LADY ELGIN" in Lake Michigan in 1860. Over 250 died with Captain Wilson in that tragedy. The 500 ton "BALTIMORE" was first through the canal down-bound and she was lost that same year of 1855 off Sheboygan, Wisconsin. The "NORTH STAR", a big steamer built in Cleveland, Ohio in 1854, took honors for being number three and she continued to ply the lakes until 1862 when she burned at her home port of Cleveland. The "SAM WARD", a steamer of 433 tons and which had been portaged over the St. Mary's Rapids into Lake Superior the year before the canal opened, came through as a member of the "first four" in 1855. She was also later converted into a barge but her eventual destiny remains unknown.

There were 153 vessel passages in the new Soo Canal in its opening year of 1855. There were 1,828 in 1870; 5,380 in 1885; 17,956 in 1895; 20,899 in 1910 and 25,407 in 1916, a peak year for the canal. The "first four" of 1855, the "ILLINOIS", "BALTIMORE", CLEVELAND" and the "SAM WARD" had no idea of what they were starting as they officially launched the new access route that brought all five of the Great Lakes together.

A couple of other "firsts" that we almost missed in looking back at the glory that grew with Lake Huron, was the advent of modern-day ship-to-shore communications and the creation of range lights as they are now known, and used, the world over.

The first marine radio broadcast of ship-to-shore data and information, (as detailed in a later chapter of this book) originated at Rogers City, Michigan in the year of 1922. A station was built there that year by Michigan Limestone and Cement Company. Its call letters were WCAF. Later, with a stronger transmitter and a call letter change to WHT, the station branched out and began serving fleets of boats on the upper lakes. In 1924 the call letters were changed for a final time to WLC and the station was licensed as a commercial marine telegraph operation. It has been on the air continuously ever since. Today it is "The Voice Of The Upper Lakes".

The range light system, used the world over by mariners and maintained by the Coast Guard throughout the United States, was created in 1860 on Lake Huron. At that time a lighthouse was operating in Bay City on the west side of the Saginaw River, near the River's mouth, having been built there in 1842 for a total investment by the government of $5,000. Dewitt C. Brawn, son of the lighthouse keeper was fifteen years old in 1860 when he conceived the idea that is today's range light system. Dewitt erected two towers in line, the front one the lower of the two, to which he attached a pulley and a line. Every evening he would place lanterns on the two towers to guide the ships into the river. He had discovered that getting the two lights to line up, one above the other, served as a perfect guide into the river. The lake captains soon caught onto the idea and used this unique plan every time they came down Saginaw Bay and into Bay City. This simple idea, created by a 15 year old Bay City boy in 1860 spread like wildfire throughout the world and is today found wherever ships sail.

Lake Huron, the strangest-shaped of all the lakes, is yet the one most frequently overlooked by the marine historian. Despite its 30,000 islands; (including "the world's largest") its unique recreational waters, the "international" aspect of its eastern shoreline along the Bruce; its thrilling sweep of 247 miles from the waters beneath the great bridge at the Straits to the whirling currents off Fort Gratiot and Port Huron; it seems to lack appeal for the statistically minded. Yet, regardless of how one looks at it, Huron *is* a BIG lake, second only to Superior in the mid-America Freshwater chain. With its entire drainage basin of 74,800 square miles, it outdistances many of the world's oceans for size. And remember, 49,500 of those square miles are Canadian, old friend.

This volume, which resulted from the author/researcher's lifetime of "living interest" in Great Lakes history, shipwrecks, lakes lore and legend, began as a survey of the records of Saginaw Bay. It was our intention to determine, if possible, how many keels this robust body of water had laid claim to over the years. Historical records showed 24 major wrecks for Saginaw Bay when we began our project. At the conclusion of our research through more than 50 books, pamphlets, newspaper stories, manuscripts and other sources, *we were able to confirm in excess of 185 shipwrecks in Saginaw Bay.* One hundred eighty-seven to be exact. History, as so unfortunately often happens, had erred. Our surprising success with Saginaw Bay encouraged us to continue our search into and through the musty old records of the balance of Lake Huron, including Georgian Bay and North Channel. The results are in this book.

Whenever possible we have given as much of a description of the wreck, its nature and its location, as we were able to ascertain with our research. In some instances there was nothing more for us to record than the bald fact that the ship was lost in Lake Huron on such and such a date. Not being divers, either professional or amateur, we accepted what the records showed. We learned that early historical marine information, like navigation aids of the same era, was more frequently than not, on the slim side.

This book contains six basic segments. The first segment, "SHIPWRECKS OF LAKE HURON", contains *all* wreck data for the entire lake as we were able to determine them. Segment two, "COMMUNICATIONS ON THE LAKES", is based on our direct reporting plus updated research support from the Federal Communications Commission in Washington, D.C. Segments on SAGINAW BAY; GEORGIAN/NORTH CHANNEL; THUNDER BAY/PRESQUE ISLE; and STRAITS OF MACKINAC are direct "lift-outs" from our overall listings as shown in Lake Huron.

While the largest concentrations of wrecks on Lake Huron will be found in the Georgian Bay/North Channel area, as well as scattered along the mouth of and deep inside Saginaw Bay, the big lake obviously affords no "safety" areas. In our research of all known and available records we have located Lake Huron shipwrecks in all areas from Saginaw Bay to Ontario's French River, from the Straits of Mackinac to the whirlpooling currents off Port Huron. Crumbling hulks of steel, iron and wood lie on Huron's bottom everywhere serving as an underwater museum to man's efforts to domesticate these waters. By their numbers we think you'll agree, Lake Huron is not to be taken lightly.

We make no claims, either historical or geographic, relative to this work. It was done in a spirit of fun and adventure as we extended a hobby that began over twenty years ago and attempted to give it the formality it deserved. We sincerely hope you will accept it in like fashion.

As some marine historians claim, there have been more than 6,000 shipwrecks in our Great Lakes since man began recording these instances of tragedy and 40% of them, these same historians state, occurred in Lake Huron. Yet this is the first single volume dedicated to this huge lake and the death, disaster and damage it has wreaked on the white man's shipping in the years since 1679.

These are the "Shipwrecks of Lake Huron...the Great Sweetwater Sea."

COMMUNICATIONS COME TO THE LAKES

As the preceding Lake Huron "disaster roster" shows, any number of vessels simply disappeared, "sailed away", "dropped through a crack in the Lake", vanished for all time as far as Great Lakes shipping history was concerned. Ship-to-shore communications were non-existent for the first 245 years that man sailed the Great Lakes, and when a ship left a port on a voyage to another destination little was known of her whereabouts, or current circumstances, until she safely reached that destination. If she did *not* appear, as so many of them obviously did not, then historians and record keepers could only assume she was gone forever. And if the GRIFFON can be considered as an example, then the "forever" designation holds a lot of water.

On April 14, 1912, a tragic accident occurred on the North Atlantic that was destined to change the communications status of shipping everywhere. On that cold, star-filled night, and with gala parties in full swing throughout the big ship, the luxurious White Star liner, TITANIC, was rushing toward New York on her maiden voyage when she struck an iceberg and plunged to the bottom, carrying more than 1,500 passengers and crew members to their death. As a direct result of this terrible accident the International Wireless Association held a convention later that year in London, England, to forge some new rules and regulations relative to ship-to-shore communications. The end result was known as "The Radio Act of 1913" requiring all vessels carrying 50 or more persons to be equipped with ship-to-shore wireless and licensed wireless operators. The Act also required standardization of the code to be transmitted, thus creating an "international" language of the telegraph keys. The United States Senate ratified the Act and it became law...On the American seas both salt and fresh.

In the Great Lakes area the first vocal reaction to the Act was heard emenating from the Rogers City area. There, in May of 1922, Michigan Limestone and Cement Company opened WCAF, a private station, to communicate with ships of the Bradley fleet as well as those owned by Boland and Cornelius Shipping Company. One old timer smilingly said the call letters stood for "We're calling a friend!" Michigan Limestone's first transmitter was a Navy surplus 500 watt spark transmitter which soon proved insufficient in range to be of any practical use. The transmitter was modified to an output of 4,000 watts, and then, encouraged by other shippers clamoring for Michigan Limestone and Cement Company to build and operate a public Radio service on the lakes, the company applied for and was granted a license by the Federal Radio Commission. Their call letters were changed from WCAF to WHT.

Prior to the opening of the 1923 navigation season, the Rogers City station learned that Radiomarine Corporation of America, (RCA), had manufactured a tube type transmitter with an output power of 1,000 watts on radiotelegraph and 500 watts on radiotelephone. They immediately leased one. The Rogers City station became the first "voice" dedicated to safety on the Great Lakes.

The steamer IRVIN L. CLYMER (then the CARL D. BRADLEY I.), was the first ship on the lakes equipped to receive the Rogers City transmissions and respond in kind. The CLYMER had a 500 watt radiotelegraph and a 250 watt radiotelephone installed on board in 1922. The Radio "voice" had come to be heard over the waters of the Great Lakes! By 1924 there were some 20 ships traveling the lakes equipped with Radio telegraphs and telephones, including the then well-known yacht, "THE OLD TIMER", flagship of the Saginaw Bay Yacht Club. That organization's clubhouse, located on the Saginaw River in Essexville, Michigan, and known at the time as the "Big City Yacht Club", was also one of the first yacht club buildings on the lakes, or elsewhere for that matter, housing complete electronic ship-to-shore communications equipment.

Oddly, in checking early historical files, it was interesting to note that early ship's masters were almost unanimously opposed to the Radiotelephone form of communications aboard their ships. It was their feeling, and frequently so stated, that this "spoken" form of communications gave too much control over the operation of the ships to the home office. These skippers voiced their approval for having all communications between shore and ship, as well as vice-versa, conducted by Radioteleghraph. Inasmuch as the Radiotelephone equipment was being leased from Radiomarine, the station returned it. This was early in the 1924 shipping season, and after the station had undergone more than two years of experiments in programming innovations designed to "showcase" their marine transmissions. These innovations had included religious services, carefully produced programs of recorded music, and a series of local, state and national "news commentaries" by the longtime Congressman for the Rogers City district, the late Fred Bradley. An occasional "live" talent program would also be featured from time to time.

The year 1924 was a memorable one for the Rogers City station. It marked the end of the experimental period of ship-to-shore and shore-to-ship voice transmissions on the lakes. It had also been the year when Robert H. Crittenden, then station manager, had designed and built a tube type transmitter that was far superior to the 10,000 watt modified U.S. Navy surplus spark transmitter in use at the time. Crittenden also constructed a version of the tube type transmitter for ships and converted the entire Bradley fleet to this system to bring greater communications to the Great Lakes. On December 20, 1924, the station changed its call letters for the third and final time, switching from WHT to WLC, the latter said to stand for "World's Limestone Center". From that last "big broadcast" of 1924, WLC remained exclusively a marine Radiotelegraph station until 1941 when "voice" again returned to the lakes.

An interesting anecdote relative to that third call letter change, and one often passed along as "gospel" by the freshwater sailormen, had William Hale (Big Bill) Thompson, Chicago's forceful and colorful mayor of that era, having a license for a Radio station in Chicago and wanting those Rogers City call letters because they were the initials of his name. A recent check of records at the Federal Communications Commission offices in Washington, D.C., failed to give any support to this story. The FCC archives indicate that the call sign, WHT, was assigned in 1924 to Press Wireless, Inc., Chicago, Illinois, for point-to-point transmission of news items by Radiotelegraphy. There was no evidence showing William Hale Thompson as licensee of this station. Another interesting WLC call sign story is that the IRVIN L. CLYMER'S first call sign was WGN, a fairly well-known signature in today's commercial Radio world. As the result of an international agreement requiring all ships to have a four letter call sign, the highly attractive three letter call, WGN, now standing for "World's Greatest Newspaper", was assigned to WGN, Inc., in Chicago in 1934.

Today, having returned to "voice" transmissions in the early 1940's, and in accordance with an international agreement that made Radiotelephone the standard safety system for the Great Lakes, WLC operates a number of satellite stations located throughout the lakes area to give a broader coverage for its services. It has ceased to operate its Radiotelegraph facilities, being the *last* station to terminate this service just as it had been first to institute it commercially on the lakes. It continues to be heard daily with its MAFORS (weather forecasts), notices to mariners, traffic messages, time signals, hydrographic informational announcements, public service broadcasts and telephone transmissions. The station handles a full schedule of marine informational exchanges for the commercial fleets plying these freshwater seas, plus an inestimable number of calls for the privately-owned recreational boats that sally forth every spring...and scoot for home every fall.

As a result of the 1973 Agreement between the United States of America and Canada for Promotion of Safety on the Great Lakes by means of Radio, (an act that was put into force May 6, 1975), WLC is a basic member of an international network for VHF broadcasting stations serving as a safety system on the Great Lakes. The WLC Radio "voice", dating back to that first pioneering effort of May, 1922, is still today the strong and vibrant link on the lakes that spells "safety" to the thousands of vessels, commercial as well as recreational, that ply these waters each year. WLC, also operating Single Side Band transmissions, (much the same as AM but without the Carrier), operates seven-days-a-week, 24 hours-a-day, ship-to-shore and shore-to-ship communications with a staff of only five full-time licensed operators and a supervisor. A modern miracle of split-second, round-the-clock, communications!

What an amazing difference there could have been in all our Great Lakes history, as well as the tragic shipwrecks that history recorded with such frightening frequency, had WLC, Rogers City and its sister stations of safety and service been on hand and on the air down through all those years since the daring Frenchman, LaSalle, saw his flagship, "GRIFFON", sail away to vanish for all time as it dropped through a crack in the lake! Unbelievable!

Today the pilot houses of our Great Lakes ships are equipped with as impressive an array of electronic communications and safety equipment as can be found anywhere in the world. Short-wave Radiotelephone, all-seeing radar, the newest in loran, automatic pilotage equipment, digital and audio depthometers, weather facsimile receivers, computers to control and report on all areas of the ship's operation. A superb collection of man's innovative ingenuity. Yet a Great Lakes storm, once it decides to turn tough, can still bottom out a behemoth...and do it in split seconds...as it did on the night of November 10, 1975. That's all it took to erase 729 feet of ship from radar screens as the "Big Fitz", the EDMUND FITZGERALD "vanished for all time".

INCREDIBLE!

SHIPWRECKS OF SAGINAW BAY

This is Saginaw Bay

Long regarded as "the most unpredictable body of water this side of the Bay of Biscay," Lake Huron's Saginaw Bay comes by that designation justifiably. With a mouth that stretches 26 miles from Au Sable Point on the north to Pte aux Barques on the south, and with a reach of 51 miles south to the Saginaw River in Bay City, it is the second largest indentation on Huron's entire shoreline.

There is an outer and an inner bay to the geographical formation of Saginaw Bay. The outer bay begins, as noted, on a line drawn from Au Sable Point to Pte aux Barques. The inner bay is that portion which lies south of Sand Point on the east and Point Lookout on the west, and which, with the Charity Islands midway between, forms a small "pocket" most frequently mis-labeled as Saginaw Bay. This inner bay is but a portion of the whole.

Many of the bay's old and historic shipwrecks were first located in the area's original survey launched in 1856 by the U.S. Army's Topographical Engineer Corps under the command of Captain George Meade. In 1863 Meade distinguished himself as the hero of the battle of Gettysburg as the commanding General in charge of all Federal forces involved in that conflict.

French explorer Rene-Robert Cavalier, Sieur de LaSalle, is generally credited with having been the first ship's captain to direct his vessel into these waters. LaSalle, who was generally following the course of

45

canoe-traveling Jean Nicolet of 50 years before, brought his ill-fated GRIFFON into the lee of the Charity Islands in 1679 to escape the fury of a Saginaw Bay storm that had hit the ship as it rounded Point aux Barques.

Many a well-known name from the pages of history tested the turbulence of Saginaw Bay's vaunted storms and wild waters. Among them were the Jesuit priest, Father Charlevoix, the French explorer, Baron of Lahonton, the gifted Englishwoman authoress, Anna Jameson, Alexander Henry, Lewis Cass, Henry Schoolcraft, Horace Greeley, Henry Wadsworth Longfellow, Samuel F.B. Morse, William Cullen Bryant, Thomas Nye and many, many others.

The "first time" skipper, on entering the bay could have been confused by the area's configuration and the two islands, Big and Little Charity, often mistakenly thought to be, "...the beginnings, or the mouth, of the bay of Saguinam." The two islands, marking access to the "inner bay", have served as colorful stepping stones in the area's growth and development. We found first mention of them in LaSalle's accountings of the voyage of the "GRIFFON" in 1679. In 1716 the French explorer "de Sabvevois" stopped at the islands enroute to Michilimackinac and found them occupied by the villages and farms of the OUTAOUSIS,* an Indian tribe of "...no fewer than 60 strong men". The OUTAOUSIS had raised grain and other crops on the fertile soil of the islands, and, according to the explorer, "...they are the most unruly and unmanageable of all the tribes in the Bay of the Saguinam." They were also visited and observed in 1721 by Father Charlevoix as he and his followers made their way up Lake Huron seeking a water route to the Pacific Ocean.

The first recorded vessel passages that traveled the

* *Some spell the tribal name as OUATOUSIS*

length of the bay and upriver to Saginaw, were the schooners SUPERIOR and DECATUR in 1822. The two ships were under Government charter transporting troops and building supplies for the new fort to be built at Saginaw City. A little over a year later the schooner RED JACKET, also under government charter, made the same trip to pick up the garrison from the fort and transport them to Detroit. The Saginaw Fort was abandoned.

John Jacob Astor's SAVAGE was the first commercial schooner to make her way down the bay from the "outside" world. She came in 1826 with a load of merchandise and started a profitable traffic between Saginaw, Bay City and several lower lake ports. The CONNEAULT PACKET, under the command of Ebeer Ward, another pioneering commercial craft, visited Saginaw Bay. The PACKET came in 1842 with a load of flour and foodstuffs, bartered for a cargo of furs, and began what was to be regarded as a hustling business between Saginaw-Bay City and the St. Clair "flats" area.

The 161 ton GOVERNOR MARCY, a small steamboat by any measurement, was the first of her breed to huff and puff her way up the Saginaw River. The year was 1836 and the little steamer had been chartered by Jennison and Little of Bay City and Saginaw. She worked the river and the bay for three years. In 1847 the GOVERNOR MARCY was wrecked near Dunkirk, New York. She was Saginaw Bay's first steamer.

Saginaw and Bay City led the way in the nation in the marketing of timber in the 1800's. Saginaw had the first *steam* sawmill. At one time there were 112 sawmills along the river between the two communities. It was once said that enough lumber was sawed in the mills on the Saginaw in one year to build a four-foot wide sidewalk that would circle the earth four times!

While Saginaw and Bay City showed how timbering was supposed to be done, the industry went sailing right up the Huron shore to poke its nose in anywhere there were trees...and where a schooner could make port. Mills sprang up at Au Gres, Sebewaing, Tawas, Au Sable, Harrisville, Black River, Alpena, Presque Isle and Cheboygan. All had their day in the world of sawdust as did the waterfront communities of Canada's Bruce Peninsula and the Georgian Bay and North Channel areas. Timbering along Lake Huron's shores had a stronger "pull" and attraction in its day than did the better-known western gold rush.

And with the timber and the river and the attraction of the "big water" at its threshold, Saginaw Bay also became known as a cradle for shipbuilding. From the earliest and most primitive yards located on the banks of the Saginaw River in the 1850's, until the final warship departed after World War II, the area contributed close to 2,000 ships of all types and descriptions to the waterways of the world. The Defoe Shipbuilding Company, last of the big yards to close in Bay City, made significant contributions to both war and peace, having built and delivered 154 warships during WWII, and almost double that number of pleasure boats and yachts. At its peak, Defoe employed 4,000 workers at its yard. Today it lies still and deserted.

In addition to the ships of commerce that were built on the Saginaw River in the 1800's, and the brawny warships built at Defoe's during World War II, Saginaw Bay has an even older claim to shipbuilding fame. Back in the 1700's, when the British were occupying many of the northern ports on Lake Huron, as well as Mackinac Island, their gunsmiths and craftsmen selected a number of locations along Saginaw Bay's western shore where they undertook the building of British Men of War, as well as other vessels. The exact number of ships completed by the British in Saginaw Bay is unknown, but the British flag and British keels were both on the waters of Lake Huron long before the American flag ever started uplake.

In 1684, shortly after LaSalle's voyage through the area, a large number of farmers and artisans from France arrived on Saginaw Bay following a voyage across the Atlantic, and a perilous trip across Canada and the United States. They settled on the rich farmland that surrounds Saginaw Bay and many of their descendants still live in the area. Bay City, in particular, reflects the Gallic influence most prominently. Five Jesuit Fathers accompanied the group carrying orders to found missions all along Lake Huron's western shore, from St. Ignace in the north to Detroit and beyond in the south. The French farmers and the artisans were obviously more successful with their objectives than were the Jesuit Fathers with their missions.

In concluding this introduction to Saginaw Bay, we can think of no better way of describing the area than repeating an old, oft-told story of how old-time lake Captains used to bring their lumber hookers down Saginaw Bay on the very darkest of nights with just their noses to lead them on. They could sniff their way safely into port, they claimed, by zeroing in on the burning sawdust odor. A story that undoubtedly ceased being told so often after 15-year old Dewitt Brawn installed the world's first range lights in Bay City in the year of 1860!

NAME OF SHIP	AREA OF LOSS	DATE
ADAIR, schr	Wrecked on Charity Island, Saginaw Bay	1886
ADDIE B., schr	Stranded near Caseville, Michigan	1888
AJAX, stmr	Burned in Saginaw Bay	1872
ALBANY, stmr	Lost in collision with PHILADELPHIA, in mouth of Saginaw Bay and mortally damaged. Crew taken aboard PHILADELPHIA which attempted to continue but with bulkheads shattered, ship sank. All crew members of both ships took to the PHILADELPHIA lifeboats and capsizings caused death of 24.	1893
ALMERSON, THOS., schr	Foundered off Pt Lookout, Saginaw Bay	1900
ANNIE MARIA, schr	Lost near Stony Island	1869
ANDOVER, schr	Stranded on Pte aux Barques Reef	1861
ANTELOPE, bge	Burned in the Saginaw River	1870
ARCTURUS, bge	Foundered in Saginaw Bay	1888
ARMSTRONG, C.W., tug	Burned on Saginaw River in Bay City	1870
AUSTIN, schr	Sank off Port Austin with the loss of 7 lives	1883
AZOV, schr	Foundered at Pte aux Barques, capsized and drifted to Chantry Island	1911
B C & CO., bge	Sank at Saginaw	1870
BARTLETT, tug	Burned on Saginaw River in Bay City	1884
BELL, DANIEL, stmr	Burned on bay near Bay City	1859
BETSCHY, JACOB, stmr	Wrecked on Port Austin Reef, Saginaw Bay	1879
BOODY, A., schr	Stranded on Pte aux Barques Reef	1887

ANTELOPE...A former schooner that had been converted into a barge and then burned on the Saginaw River in 1885.

NAME OF SHIP	AREA OF LOSS	DATE
BROWN, WILLIE, tug	Burned on the river in East Saginaw	1889
BUCEPHELUS, prop	Foundered on the bay with 10 lives lost	1854
BUCEPHELUS, schr	Sank on the bay	1879
BUCKINGHAM, schr	Lost in Saginaw Bay	1870
CARDINGTON, M.D., schr	Wrecked off Au Sable Point	1873
CHALLENGE, tug	Burned on the river in East Saginaw	1880
CHERUB, ycht	Burned and sank on river in Bay City	1974
CLEVELAND, prop	Burned off Charity Islands	1880
COAST GUARD CUTTER 40'	Sank at Gravelly Shoal	1967
COBURN, R.G., stmr	Foundered near Pte aux Barques, 32 lives lost	1871
COE, S.S., tug	Burned and sank near Port Austin	1876
COMAN, L.D., schr	Wrecked at Pte aux Barques	1865
CRISPIN, brig	Stranded at Pte aux Barques	1853
CURLEW, schr	Foundered in river at Saginaw	1890
CYCLONE, bge	Lost at Alabaster (former steamer PITTSBURGH)	1885
CYGNET, bge	Exploded and burned in Saginaw Bay	1875
DAVIS, GEORGE, schr	Ashore in Saginaw Bay	1901
DEER, tug	Burned and sank off Au Gres	1908
DESPATCH, tug	Wrecked on Pte aux Barques Reef	1871
DETROIT II, stmr	Collision with Brig. NUCLEUS, sank, Saginaw Bay	1854
DETROIT, CITY OF, prop	Sank in bay with all hands lost (20)	1863
DICKENSON, GEO. B., tug	Lost in collision on bay near Bay City	1886
DOBBINS, ANNA, tug	Foundered in bay near Charity Islands	1886

CAPITOLA...125' steam yacht built in Toledo and owned by H.T. Wickes of Saginaw, Michigan. Left high and dry in the Saginaw River as result of the "Memorial Day" storm of 1940 - she was sold to a banana shipping company by Lloyds of London and foundered in Gulf of Mexico.

NAME OF SHIP	AREA OF LOSS	DATE
DORMER, bge	Sank in Saginaw River near Crow Island	1940
DORR, E.P., tug	Collision in Saginaw Bay, sank	1856
DREADNAUGHT, schr	Collision near Au Gres, salvaged	1886
DREW, GEO. L., schr	Wrecked at Charity Island	1866
DUDLEY, dredge	Foundered in bay off Au Sable Point	1934
DUNLAP, GEO. L., stmr	Sunk by ice on bay 14 miles from Bay City	1880
EAGLE, tug	Burned on Saginaw Bay	1869
EMERALD, bge	Sank in Saginaw River, total loss	1880
ENTERPRISE, stmr	Foundered off Pte aux Barques, many lost	1883

NAME OF SHIP	AREA OF LOSS	DATE
ESPERANCE, schr	Sank in freak storm, (one of first locally built vessels that have been traced to Louis Tromble in 1788)	1842
EUGENE, schr	Wrecked in storm, Port Austin Reef	1867
EUREKA, slp	Wrecked off Au Sable Point	1869
EVENING STAR, stmr	Sank in bay near Gravelly Shoal	1841
EVERETT, A.E., schr	Foundered north of Pte aux Barques in ice	1895
EXCELSIOR, schr	Burned on Saginaw River	1869
FERGUSON, bge	Sank at East Tawas	1886
FERRIS, B.F., stmr	Burned at Caseville	1891
FLETCHER, KATE, tug	Burned on the river in Saginaw	1877
FORBES, CHRISTIAN, tug	Burned on the river near Bay City	1895
FOSTER, A.M., prop	Foundered in bay near Pte aux Barques	1888
GARDEN CITY, stmr	Burned 4 miles from Bay City	1903
GIANT, tug	Sank in Saginaw River	1894
GLOBE, stmr	Burned on Saginaw Bay (raised and made a barge)	1863
GLOBE, mv	Foundered in Saginaw Bay	1954
GOVERNOR SMITH, stmr	Collision off Pte aux Barques	1906
GREEN BAY, CITY OF, stmr	Burned and sank on Saginaw Bay	1909
GROVER, CHRIS, schr	Stranded near Au Sable (later sank in Superior)	1880
HALE, E.B., prop	Foundered in Saginaw Bay, crew saved by NEBRASKA	1897
HANNA, HOWARD, stmr	Foundered on Port Austin Reef (later raised)	1913
HECTOR, schr	Foundered in Saginaw Bay	1903

NAME OF SHIP	AREA OF LOSS	DATE
HERCULES, *dredge*	Sank east of Tawas Lignt, south of Oscoda	1932
HOLT, GEO. W., *schr*	Stranded on Port Austin Reef	1880
HUNTER SAVIDGE, *schr*	Lost off Pte aux Barques, 5 lives lost	1899
HURON, *stmr*	Foundered off Port Austin Reef	1861
HYDE, H., *bge*	Lost off Pointe aux Barques	1883
IRON CHIEF, *stmr*	Foundered off Pointe aux Barques	1904
JACKSON, ANDREW, *schr*	Foundered off Pointe aux Barques	1901
JOHNSON, LEVI, *tug*	Exploded and burned on river, 4 lives lost	1867
JOHNSON, WILLARD, *schr*	Foundered off Pointe aux Barques	1865
JOSEPH, *bge*	Lost near Caseville	1885
KELLER, WILLIAM, *schr*	Collision off Au Sable Point in bay	1888
KEOSAGAS, *stmr yht*	Burned at mouth of Saginaw River	1916
KEYSTONE STATE, *stmr*	Foundered in bay, 33 lives lost	1861
KIMBALL, S.H., *schr*	Sank in collision with steamer G. STONE, NW of Pte aux Barques, crew saved	1895
KING, CHAS. A., *schr*	Foundered near Pte aux Barques, crew saved	1885
LAMBERT, R.T., *schr*	Stranded near Caseville	1873
LANGELL BOYS, *stmr*	Burned south of Au Sable in Saginaw Bay	1931
LEE, FREDERICK, *tug*	Foundered NE of Pte aux Barques, 5 lives lost	1936
LIKEN, CHAS. W., *stmr*	Burned on river in Bay City	1905
LINDEN, *stmr*	Burned and sank in Tawas Bay	1923

NAME OF SHIP	AREA OF LOSS	DATE
MADDEN, LIZZIE, stmr	Burned off Point Lookout	1907
MAGIC, schr	Sank in bay (later raised)	1861
MAIME, scow	Foundered near Pte aux Barques	1858
MARGARET, ycht	Burned in Essexville	1924
MASON, L.G., stmr	Burned on Saginaw River, Bay City	1886
MASSILON, schr	Foundered N of Pte aux Barques	1876
MATOA, stmr	Stranded on reef at Port Austin, (raised)	1913
MAYO, NELLIE, tug	Burned near Saginaw	1870
McDONALD, CHAS. A., tug	Burned on river in Saginaw	1893
McLEAN, ANDREW A., tug	Foundered SE of Tawas in Saginaw Bay	1916
MELBOURNE, stmr	Sank in river at Bay City	1918
MERCHANT, schr	Wrecked at Pte aux Barques, 5 lives lost	1849

MATOA...Propellor freighter of 2,311 g.t., built in Cleveland in 1890... shoaled on Port Austin Reef in "big storm" of 1913.

NAME OF SHIP	AREA OF LOSS	DATE
METROLOPE, stmr	Sank north of Port Austin on the bay	1903
MICHIGAN, brig	Wrecked on reef at Pte aux Barques	1870
MILLER, E.M., tug	Burned on river	1874
MINER, JULIA, schr	Lost east of Pte aux Barques	1894
MINER, J.J., schr	Total loss at Caseville	1877
MINOR, JOHN, schr	Lost west of Pte aux Barques	1902
MIRANDA, schr	Wrecked on Port Austin Reef	1871
MOHAWK, stmr	Former Reserve Cutter, Lost at Pte aux Barques	1870
MOHEGAN, brig	Sank at Pte aux Barques	1870
MONA, schr	Lost off Pte aux Barques, all hands lost	1887
MONTEZUMA, brig	Lost in collision above Pte aux Barques	1902
MONTICELLO, schr	Lost near Port Austin	1904
MONTMORENCY, schr	Wrecked at Charity Islands	1901
MOORE, W.A., tug	Sank in Saginaw Bay squall	1871
MORRELL, DANIEL, stmr	Foundered north of Port Austin, 28 lives lost	1966
MUNSON, ISAAC, schr	Stranded near Caseville	1888
NAIAD, stmr	Sank off Pte aux Barques (later raised)	1911
NEILSEN, EMMA L., schr	Collision 11 miles N of Pte aux Barques, sank	1911
NELL, LITTLE, stmr	Exploded on river at City of Saginaw	1862
NEPTUNE, stmr	Burned on river at East Saginaw	1874
OCEAN, schr	Foundered at Tawas in bay	1873
ORION, schr	Foundered at Pte aux Barques Reef (later sank, 1861)	1856
OWEN, tug	Burned at Tawas	1921

NAME OF SHIP	AREA OF LOSS	DATE
PARANA, bark	Lost in heavy storm on bay	1863
PATTER, H.C., stmr	Total loss in heavy gale on Saginaw Bay	1891
PHILADELPHIA, stmr	Collision with ALBANY in fog, 24 lives lost	1893
PIERCE, MARY E., tug	Stranded at Au Sable	1906
PILOT, schr	Collision near Caseville	1896
QUEEN CITY, bge	1,000 "tonner" lost at Pte aux Barques	1866
RACINE, schr	Wrecked near Pte aux Barques Reef	1892
REBECCA, schr	Sank off Detour, raised & resank off Alabaster	1872
REDFERN, oil screw	Foundered off Tawas Point	1930
REEVES, KITTY, schr	Lost in Saginaw Bay near Tawas Point	1870
REID, KATE, tug	Burned on the river in city of Saginaw	1873
RELIEF, tug	Burned on the Saginaw River	1867
REYNOLDS, GEO. W., stmr	Burned in the river at Bay City	1872
ROCKET, schr	Collision 10 miles north of Pte aux Barques	1860
ROEN, MARQUIS, stmr	Burned on the river in Bay City	1932
RUELLE, GRACE, stmr	Lost near Port Austin on the bay	1899
ROSEDALE, stmr	Wrecked on Charity Island	1897
RURAL, schr	Stranded near Caseville on the bay	1873
SACRAMENTO, stmr	Foundered on reef off Port Austin	1917
SALINA, stmr	Sank in collision with LIZZIS LAW, near Bay City	1895

NAME OF SHIP	AREA OF LOSS	DATE
SANTIAGO, schr	Lost in bay near Pte aux Barques	1918
SEA GULL, bge	Burned at the Tawas docks (built in 1864 as a schooner, sailed to Africa in '66 as a brig, made barge same year)	1888
SEA GULL, tug	Sank in Saginaw Bay following collision off Linwood	1889
SEA GULL, prop	Burned at Tawas	1890
SEATON, L., schr	Lost near Pte aux Barques and totaled	1892
SHAW, JOHN, schr	Lost near Au Sable Point	1894
SMITH, H.P., tug	Burned on the Saginaw River	1872
SMOKE, KITTIE, tug	Burned at the mouth of the Saginaw River	1889
SOUTHWESTERN, schr	Lost in collision off Pte aux Barques	1850
ST. CLAIR, schr	Foundered at Pte aux Barques Reef	1855
STAR, tug	Burned on the river at City of Saginaw	1869

JOHN SHAW...schooner of 928 g.t., built in 1885 in West Bay City... Lost in gale near Au Sable Point, Saginaw Bay in 1894.

NAME OF SHIP	AREA OF LOSS	DATE
STOCKMAN, H.D., schr	Lost in squall on the bay	1894
STRANGER, schr	Stranded near Caseville	1873
SUMMIT, schr	Stranded off Tawas Point	1872
SUPERIOR, bge	Wrecked at Oak Point in the bay	1895
SWAN, tug	Burned on the river in East Saginaw	1875
TABLE ROCK, bge	Foundered off Tawas Point	1872
TIGER, tug	Burned on the river in Bay City	1875
TOLEDO, tug	Lost on the river in Bay City	1880
TRAFFIC, stmr	Total wreck near Sebewaing	1868
TRAFFIC, tug	Burned on river in Saginaw	1869
TROY, stmr	Foundered in Saginaw Bay with 23 lives lost	1859
UNION, tug	Burned and sank in the bay	1870
VALENTINE, schr	Lost on reef at Port Austin	1873
VENICE, CITY OF, stmr	Sank in collision on Saginaw Bay	1902
VICTOIRE, MARIE, schr	Lost in squall in bay	1887
VOLUNTEER, schr	Foundered on reef at Port Austin, crew saved	1893
WARD, J.P., stmr	Burned on river in Bay City and later rebuilt	1865
WATERWITCH, prop	Lost in bay, all 28 lives lost	1863
WAURECAN, bge	Foundered on reef at Port Austin	1875
WAVE, stmr	Burned at Charity Islands	1874
WAYNE, schr	Stranded at Au Sable Point	1875
WESLEY, JOHN, schr	Lost at Pte aux Barques	1894
WESTOVER, stmr	Burned on AuGres River	1881
WHITE, KIRK, schr	Foundered in Saginaw Bay storm	1869
WHITE SQUALL, schr	Collision in bay with 7 lives lost	1872

NAME OF SHIP	AREA OF LOSS	DATE
WILCOX, O., tug	Foundered off Tawas Point, sank in 7 minutes	1893
WILLIAMS, C.P., brig	Lost in storm near Port Austin	1886
WIMAN, schr	Lost on Pte aux Barques Reef	1855
WITCH, tug	Sank in storm on bay	1869
WITCH OF THE WEST, tug	Burned in the bay off the mouth of the river	1904
WYOMING, stmr	Foundered off Port Austin	1904

SHIPWRECKS OF GEORGIAN BAY, NORTH CHANNEL

Welcome To The Georgian—And Its North Channel
Often considered "the sixth Great Lake", the Georgian is actually the body of water that Champlain discovered in 1615, and which he dubbed, "Mer Douce". Loosely translated, this becomes "The Sweetwater Sea". Champlain, while credited with being the discoverer of Lake Huron, did *not* see the main body of the lake.

And the Georgian truthfully is a sea. It is 125 miles long, 55 miles wide, and it measures 549 feet in depth at its deepest sounding. That's considerably larger than many of the water areas of the world that are officially known as "seas".

While the French came in the 1600's, (and the Jesuit Fathers were a part of their fabric of settlement), in the 18th century, the Georgian experienced the same mysterious disappearance of the white man, as well as white man's history, as did Manitoulin Island on its western shore. During the 1700's little happened, and little is known of either the bay or the huge island. It took the War of 1812 to rekindle the flame of liberty and freedom once again in the Georgian, for here, unlike moody Manitoulin, the War *did* play a role. Much of the British action in the midwest during this war... concerned itself with the Georgian. Today, as a result of this war, the history of England, Canada and the United States shall be forever inter-mingled in the waters of the "sixth Great Lake".

The towns, villages, and communities that sprung into being on the Georgian in the 1800's all seemed to host shipyards, and the smell of damp lumber, paint, oakum, and sawdust, put an unmistakable tang in the air as these towns put ships in the water. There were forests everywhere and Georgian Bay home ports were painted, etched or carved on their transoms.

Early ships built on the Georgian were jacks-of-all-trades, as they fished the deep waters of the bay and Lake Huron for the fat trout and whitefish; carted cargo-holds full of hardware and farming implements up and down the Canadian coast; ferried lumberjacks to Ontario's logging camps and then transported their lumber to the world; carried passengers and freight and household goods and anything and everything that needed moving to anywhere it needed to *be* moved. It was the age of sail on the Georgian and they were all there; sloop rigs, yawls, mackinaw boats, schooners, brigs and barks, tall ships and lean ships, and few and far between the navigational aids, channel markers and detailed charts today's mariner takes for granted. In 1868 there were 1,875 sailing ships listed on the lakes. And then, as the years passed, so too did the sailboat. And the steamboat came to the Georgian to take its place.

Actually, the very first steamers came to the Georgian around mid-century when the MAZEPPA and KALOOLAH and the small GORE were brought in to make freight runs out of Owen Sound and Collingwood to Parry Sound and French River and Killarney and the Manitoulin. In fact, it is the little GORE that is today generally credited with being the source for the name of Manitoulin's seat of government. On a late fall trip in North Channel the 149 ton GORE had to take refuge from a nasty storm by ducking into a large cove on Manitoulin's north shore. Before the GORE could make her way to return to her home port, winter arrived and she was trapped in the ice.....and she remained there all winter long, solidly frozen in. Settlers in and around Kagawong would occasionally walk over to see the little steamer, as well as her crew, stranded in the ice in the bay. Eventually, and quite naturally, the cove/bay became known as "GORE BAY", and today it is the name of the prosperous and popular community, on the shores of the bay, that serves as the seat of all Manitoulin governmental function. It is thus that fame is sometimes created.

As any of today's mariners know, and as many a visiting yachtsman has discovered, much to his discomfort and dismay, Georgian Bay is filled with scores of surprisingly vicious and cleverly camouflaged shoals and reefs. Additionally, its eastern and northern shores are accented with a rash of rock-encrusted islands whose numbers in the thousands defy accurate count. And Georgian Bay storms, as they originate in the east and/or northeastern quadrants, are known for their ability to make strong seamen blanch. They have laid many a good ship, as well as her crew, to permanent rest beneath her raging waters. The following extracts from our master list of Lake Huron wrecks give proof of this brute power.

North Channel, perhaps because of its more protected form, running as it generally does, east and west between the Ontario shore and Manitoulin Island, has suffered a lower percentage of wrecks than has its source, the Georgian. But wrecks there have been, and strandings and burnings, and we've tried to track down as many of them as possible based on the research and data available to us. *We sincerely believe that the following list is the most comprehensive of the Georgian and North Channel that is available today from any one source.*

NAME OF SHIP	AREA OF LOSS	DATE
ABIGAIL, schr	Sank in storm on Georgian	1892
ADA, schr	Sank at Collingwood	1859
ADVANCE, stmr	Wrecked at Manitoulin Island	1927
AFRICA, prop	Sank in storm near Cove Island, 13 lives lost	1895
AFRICA, stmr	Burned at Owen Sound	1886
AGAWA, stmr	Stranded at Manitoulin Island	1927
ALASKA, stmr	Sank near Tobermory	1910
ALEXANDRIA, stmr	Burned at Little Current	1927
ALGOMA, stmr	Sank at Collingwood (formerly City of Toronto & Racine, not to be confused wth Algoma wrecked in 1885 on Superior with loss of 38 lives)	1870
ALICE G., stmr tug	Sank near Tobermory	1927

AFRICA...Canadian propeller passenger-freight packet of 482 g.t., built in Kingston, New York in 1887...foundered near Cove Island in Georgian Bay in 1895 with 13 lives lost.

NAME OF SHIP	AREA OF LOSS	DATE
ALVA D., tug	Burned in Beaverstone Bay	1914
ARABIA, schr	Lost in Georgian Bay near Echo Island	1884
ARIEL, schr	Wrecked near Collingwood	1870
ASIA, stmr	Sank in heavy storm, Georgian Bay, 123 lives lost	1882
ATHABASCA, stmr	Foundered near Lonely Island	1910
ATLANTIC, stmr	Burned in lee of Pancake Islands north of Parry Sound	1903
ATWATER, S.T., schr	Wrecked on Manitoulin Island	1895
BALTIC, prop	Burned at Collingwood (former FRANCIS SMITH)	1896
BAVARIAN, schr	Stranded 1 mile south of Cape Smith, crew of 8 saved by Indians from Manitoulin Island	1898
BELLE, stmr	Foundered in storm, position unknown	1852
BENTLEY, JOHN, schr	Sank from a white squall on the bay	1886
BISHOP, H.B., schr	Foundered in severe storm on the bay	1882
BONNIE DOON, slp	Burned at Meldrum Bay	1880
BOWMAN, C.M.	Wrecked near Vail's Point on the bay	1915
BRECK, MARY L., schr	Wrecked near Tobermory	1900
BRODER, ELIZABETH, schr	Wrecked on Manitoulin	18---
BRUCE MINES, stmr	Foundered off Cape Hurd with all hands lost	1854
BUCKEYE, bge	Burned and sank on the bay	1885
BUCKLEY, EDWARD, stmr	Burned at Manitoulin Island	1929
BURLINGTON, prop	Burned at Meldrum Bay (built in Bay City)	1895
CAHOON, THOS. H., schr	Sank at Innes Island, (built 1881, West Saginaw)	1913

NAME OF SHIP	AREA OF LOSS	DATE
CAMPBELL, P.M., tug	Burned at Manitoulin Island	1898
CANADIAN, schr	Foundered near Clara Island in the Whalesback	1880
CASCADEN, schr	Foundered near Tobermory	1871
CASTALIA, brig	Capsized and sank in violent bay storm	1871
CHAMBERLAIN, stmr	Wrecked on bay	1901
CHINA, schr	Sank near Cape Hurd	1883
CITY QUEEN, tug	Lost in Georgian Bay	1924
CLARK, JAMES, tug	Burned at Owen Sound	1896
CLEMENT, N.P., stmr	Scuttled in Georgian Bay	1968
CLEVELAND, CITY OF, stmr	Burned and sank off Perserverance Island	1901
COLLINGWOOD, schr	Burned at Byng Inlet	1878
COLLINGWOOD, CITY OF, stmr	Burned at the Wharf in Collingwood	1905
CONSUELO, schr	Wrecked off Marble Head (salvaged)	1885
CRANAGE, THOS., stmr	Wrecked and total loss on Watcher's Reef	1911
CREAM CITY, stmr	Wrecked, Wheeler's Reef with 2 schooners in tow	1918
CREOLE, tug	Burned on the Wye River	1905
DAVIDSON, FRED, tug	Sank at Point au Baril	1916
DUFFERIN, LADY, schr	Wrecked on Dufferin Point	1886
DUNCAN CITY, schr	Lost in North Channel, Frazer Bay, Baie Finn area	1888
EASTNOR, stmr	Burned at Wiarton	1933
ELITE, tug	Burned at Jennie Island	1933
EMILY, schr	Total wreck in bay storm	1858
EMMA, tug	Burned in Georgian Bay near Sister Rock Beacon	1912
ENTERPRISE, schr	Foundered near Barrie Island, North Channel	1903

GARIBALDI...Canadian-built schooner lost in Georgian Bay in 1865... 4 lives lost.

NAME OF SHIP	AREA OF LOSS	DATE
ESPERANZA, slp	Burned at Cape Croker	1907
EVA, tug	Burned on Linsay Bank, 3/4 mile N. of Drummond Island	1881
FOREST CITY, bge	Wrecked at Bear's Rump near Tobermory	1904
GAME, schr	Lost on bay near Collingwood in storm	1871
GARIBALDI, schr	Foundered in bay storm with 4 lives lost	1865
GARY D., tug	Burned near Strawberry Island	1958
GEORGIAN, stmr	Foundered near Owen Sound in bay storm	1884
GERMANIC, stmr	Burned at Collingwood	1917
GETWORK, stmr	Burned at Collingwood	1917
GIDLEY, J.G., tug	Burned near Meldrum Bay	1909
GILPHIE, stmr	Burned at Lion's Head	1909
GLENSTRIVEN, stmr	Wrecked on the bay in storm	1923
GOLDEN FISHER	Burned off Cape Hurd	1943
GOLDEN WEST, schr	Foundered in storm near Snake Island	1884
GORE, stmr	Dismantled after years of service	1880
GRAND RAPIDS, CITY OF, stmr	Burned at Tobermory	1907
HACKETT, ALICE, schr	Total loss near Fitzwilliam Island	1828
HELEN B., tug	Lost in storm near Gull Island	1936
HIBOU, stmr	Sank near Squaw Point, 7 lives lost	1936
HOLLAND, schr	Broke up on Wheeler's Reef, False Detour	1918
HOPE, schr	Lost in bay squall	1858
HOPE, slp	Foundered near St. Joesph's Island	1804
IMPERIAL, schr	Lost after capsizing in storm	1889

J.M. JENKS...Steamer of Canadian registery lost in 1913 near Midland in Georgian Bay.

NAME OF SHIP	AREA OF LOSS	DATE
INDIA, stmr	Burned and sank near West Mary Island	1928
IROQUOIS, tug	Burned and sank in McBean Channel	1906
IROQUOIS, stmr	Wrecked and burned at Spanish Mills	1908
JENKS, J.M., stmr	Total loss near Midland, year of BIG storm	1913
JONAS, schr	Sank after collision in Georgian	1898
JONES, J.H., stmr	Foundered near Lion's Head, 26 lives lost	1906
KIDD, JOSEPHINE, prop	Burned and lost from fire on the bay	1882
KINCARDINE, prop	Lost on French River	1888
KING, FOREST, schr	Lost in Georgian Bay, sank due to storm violence	1869
KING, JAMES, schr	Wrecked and sank near Tobermory	1901

NAME OF SHIP	AREA OF LOSS	DATE
LADY OF THE LAKE, stmr	Sank after collision at Christian Island	1911
LANCASTER, bge	Lost in Bayfield Sound	1907
LEE, JOHN, SR., stmr	Burned at Pt. McNicol	1913
LEE, LAURA, tug	Burned at Meldrum Bay	1929
LEWIS, SAM, prop	Sank off Cape Croker	1871
LISGAR, schr	Wrecked near Cove Island	1899
LONDON, CITY OF, stmr	Burned in Collins Inlet	1875
LONG, JOHN, tug	Burned at Meldrum Bay	1900
LOWELL, brig	Sank near Cove Island	1871
LUCKNOW, stmr	Burned at Midland	1935
LUCKPORT, tug	Burned at Midland	1934
LUFF, SOPHIA L., schr	Wrecked in the Georgian	1892
MAGNETTEWAN, prop	Wrecked at Byng Inlet, ashore	1897
MANISOO, stmr	Foundered in gale force storm, 16 lives lost	1928
MANITOULIN, stmr	Burned near Manitowaning, 30 lives lost	1882
MAZEPPA, stmr	Wrecked off the Saugeen	1856
MAPLEDAWN, stmr	Foundered at Christian Island	1924
MARTIN, C.C., tug	Foundered at Key Harbour	1911
MARTIN, JOHN, tug	Lost in storm in Georgian Bay	1890
MARY ANN, tug	Lost in Georgian Bay, 2 lives lost	1883
MAYFLOWER, stmr	Burned at Penetanguishene	1900
McBRIER, A.J., stmr	Burned on Georgian Bay	1907
McKERRAL, P.R., stmr	Burned at Collingwood	1878
McLEOD, JANE, schr	Lost near Parry Sound	1890
McPHEE, BELLE, schr	Foundered near Thornbury	1854
McVIE, MARY, prop	Foundered at Walker's Point, Manitoulin	1878

NAME OF SHIP	AREA OF LOSS	DATE
MEAFORD, CITY OF, stmr	Burned at Collingwood	1919
METAMORA, tug	Burned off Parry Sound	1890
METEOR, stmr	Wrecked at Spanish River	1883
MICHIGAN, stmr	Foundered off Hope Island	1943
MICHIPICOTEN, prop	Burned at Cock's Dock, Bayfield Sound (also listed as E.K. ROBERTS)	1927
MIDLAND CITY, stmr	Burned at Midland	1955
MIDLAND, CITY OF, stmr	Burned at Collingwood	1916
MILLER, JANE, stmr	Wrecked at Colpoy Bay, 30 lives lost	1881
MILTON, JOE, tug	Burned in Georgian Bay	1904
MINCH, CHAS. P., schr	Lost near Cove Island	1898
MORRISON, A.H., stmr	Foundered off Christian Island	1902
MOUNTAINEER, schr	Stranded following Georgian Bay storm	1864

JANE MILLER...Small passenger-freight packet built in 1878 at Crops Yard in Little Current, Ontario...sunk with all hands, in Colpoy Bay in 1881.

NAME OF SHIP	AREA OF LOSS	DATE
MYSTERY, stmr	Burned on the Georgian	1911
MYSTIC, tug	Foundered at Cockburn Island	1878
NANCY, H.M.S., schr	Burned on Nancy Island (now Museum)	1814
NEECHEE, schr	Wrecked on Russell Island near Tobermory	1863
NESSEN, N.J., stmr	Foundered near Meaford (salvaged, sank 1929)	1919
NEWAGO, stmr	Lost in storm near Tobermory	1903
NORTH WIND, stmr	Sank northeast of Clapperton Island, south of Crocker Island	1926
NORTHERN BELLE, prop	Burned at Byng Inlet	1898

NORTHERN BELLE...Canadian propeller of 290 g.t., built in Marine City in 1875...burned at Byng Inlet in Georgian Bay in 1898.

NAME OF SHIP	AREA OF LOSS	DATE
OKENZA, tug	Burned at docks in Wiarton	1878
OLD CONCORD, bge	Foundered in storm off Lion's Head	1888
OREGON, stmr	Wrecked and burned near Thessalon	1908
OPHIR, tug	Burned at Parry Sound	1919
OSBORNE, J.M., prop	Sank after collision near Owen Sound	1884
OSPREY, tug	Burned on the Georgian	1895
OWEN SOUND, CITY OF, prop	Wrecked at Clapperton Island (raised and lost later in Lake Huron as the SATURN)	1887
PACIFIC, prop	Burned at Collingwood docks, towed out and sunk	1898
PARRY SOUND, CITY OF, stmr	Burned at Collingwood	1900
PEARL, schr	Wrecked on East Sister Reef	1855
PEASE, EDWARD, stmr	Burned at Collingwood	1904
PEG, tug	Wrecked on Cockburn Island	1878
PILOT, tug	Burned on Moon River	1910
PLOUGHBOY, stmr	Burned on the Georgian (as T.F. PARKS)	1879
QUEBEC, stmr	Foundered on Magnetic Reef, (later raised and sank in St. Mary's River)	1878
REED, FRANK, tug	Wrecked near Barrie Island	1899
REGINA, schr	Lost near Cove Island	1881
REID, JAMES, prop	Foundered near Byng Inlet	1917
ROBERTS, E.K., prop	Burned at Cook's Dock, Bayfield Sound under name MICHIPICOTEN	1927
ROBERT, K., tug	Burned at Tobermory	1935
ROBERTSON, MARY R.	Burned at Byng Inlet	1878
ROSE, schr	Lost in Georgian Bay	1851
RUSSEL ROQUE, tug	Burned at Gore Bay	1931

NAME OF SHIP	AREA OF LOSS	DATE
SALVOR, stmr	Foundered off Manitoulin in bay	1917
SARONIC, stmr	Burned at Cockburn Island	1916
SAUCY JIM, tug	Burned near Christian Island	1910
SAYMO, tug	Lost near Club Island	1935
SCHOOLCRAFT, stmr	Burned at Midland	1920
SCOTT, THOS. R., stmr	Lost off Cabot's Head	1914
SCOVILLE, PHILO, schr	Wrecked near Tobermory	1889
SEA HORSE, schr	Stranded at Fitzwilliam Island	1871
SEA QUEEN, tug	Burned at Meldrum Bay	1932
SECRET, prop	Burned at Star Shoal	1871
SEYMOUR, WM., stmr	Foundered near Lonely Island	1876
SEVERN, schr	Wrecked at Cove Island	1895
SHANDON, schr	Lost in Wingfield Basin	1884
SHANNON, schr	Foundered in bay storm	1870
SHERWOOD, NELLIE, schr	Foundered near Cabot Head, all hands lost	1882
SHICKLUNA, prop	Sank near Algoma Mills	1883
SIGNAL, stmr	Burned at Midland	1905
SILVERSPRAY, stmr	Burned at Owen Sound	1877
SMITH, ELLA, tug	Sank at French River	1895
SON & HEIR, schr	Foundered in bay, total loss, (first big storm)	1869
SOPHIA, schr	Lost in Georgian Bay	1854
STANLEY, scow	Foundered in bay storm	1859
STAR, schr	Sank in bay storm with 6 lives lost	1852
STARLIGHT, schr	Burned on the bay with 4 lives lost	1883
STEVENS, O., bark	Wrecked and lost in bay storm	1867
SURPRISE, tug	Burned in the bay	1905

NAME OF SHIP	AREA OF LOSS	DATE
SWEEPSTAKES, schr	Sank in the Big Tub, Tobermory	1896
TELEGRAM, stmr	Burned at Fitzwilliam Island	1908
TEMPEST II, stmr	Burned in Parry Sound	1909
THOMPSON, EMMA E., stmr	Burned at Enola Island	1914
TORRENT, JOHN, tug	Burned at Richards Landing	1913
TRANSLAKE #3	Capsized in Georgian Bay	1958
TURRET CROWN, stmr	Stranded near Meldrum-Britomart Point (salvaged)	1924
TURNER, ALVIN, stmr	Burned on the Georgian	1905
VANDERBILT, bge	Burned near Serpent Island	1882
VICTORIA, tug	Foundered in Georgian Bay	1896
VITA, ycht	Lost off Yeo Island	1910
WALTERS, JOHN, schr	Sank near Russell Island	1899
WARD, MARY, stmr	Lost near Collingwood on Nottawasaga Shoal	1872
WATERLOO, stmr	Wrecked in the Georgian	1846
WATTS, J.G.	Foundered on Devil's Island Shoal	1895
WAUBUNO, stmr	Wreckage and capsized hull found near Moose Point, 30 lives lost (some estimates as High as 70)	1858
WAUSEDA II, tug	Burned at Fitzwilliam Island	1948
WAWINET, tug	Lost south of Beausoleil Island	1942
WESTERN STAR, stmr	Wrecked on Clapperton Island	1915
WESTFORD, stmr	Burned at John Island	1904
WETMORE, W.L., stmr	Wrecked on Russell Island	1901
WINDSLOW, stm bge	Burned at Meldrum Bay	1910
WINNANA, prop	Burned at Tobermory - mail boat	1909
WINNIPEG, CITY OF, stmr	Lost in fire on the bay	1881
WINONA, stmr	Burned at Spragge	1929

NAME OF SHIP	AREA OF LOSS	DATE
WINSLOW, KATE, schr	Sank at Meldrum Bay (salvaged and later lost in 1897 in Lake Michigan)	1881
WOLF, LOTTIE, schr	Foundered near north shore of Hope Island (now a reef)	1879
WOLSEY, GENERAL, stmr	Burned on the Georgian, near Cape Croker	1886
WOODRUFF, J.S., schr	Wrecked in storm on bay and sank	1886
YORK STATE, schr	Foundered on the bay	1886

SHIPWRECKS OF THUNDER BAY... MIDDLE ISLAND...FALSE PRESQUE ISLE AND PRESQUE ISLE

Thunder Bay - Presque Isle... Lake Huron's "Wreck Alley"

A close check of the marine records and disaster tallies for Lake Huron will promp any researcher to look sharply, and in detail, at that stretch of water that embraces Thunder Bay on the south to Presque Isle on the north. Reason? Because these locations, as well as Middle Island and False Presque Isle, appear in the Lake Huron historical records with such amazing frequency. Assembling all available data on these areas under one heading, the theory becomes factual, these are obviously dangerous waters!

Since the inception of marine record-keeping, 124 major disasters have occurred in this innocent-appearing stretch of Lake Huron's sparkling blue waters. Over 100 major wrecks, sinkings, strandings, burnings, collisions, plus an incomplete tally of human casualties, make this one of the tougher, touchier freshwater cruising areas of the lakes. It is a passage that merits all the respect a skipper can muster as he moves through its waters.

Thunder Bay itself, because of its geographical position on lower Michigan's eastern coastline, has long been noted for its intemperate and frequently unpredictable nature. Laying as it does astride the 45th Parallel, directly across the lake from Canada's Stokes Bay, and at a point where the Michigan shoreline begins to fall away to the west at a farily rapid rate, Thunder Bay may have a geographical right to its age-old reputation as a "tough corner" on the north-south shipping lane. Additionally, during the boom period of the Michigan timbering industry, one of the giant log rafts used by lumbering firms to get their logs to market, broke up in a storm here and spewed over two million feet of lethal timber into these waters. Some of these maverick logs are still a menace to small boats today as they lurk beneath the surface in the form of water-logged deadheads.

The passage from Thunder Bay to Presque Isle has been noteworthy since man first began sailing these waters. Father Hennepin noted it in the log he kept aboard the Griffon on that ill-fated vessel's voyage uplake in 1679. In 1837, Thomas Nye, a well-known journalist and historian of the period, recorded his impressions of a trip through the area aboard the CONSTELLATION. "A very strong sea and head wind caught us as we were crossing the bay and our boat tossed and rolled very much all night." He later noted in his journal that the steamer had laid-to off Presque Isle for seven hours as wood scows scurried back and forth from shore transporting needed fuel supplies. The price was $3.00 a cord, Nye wrote, and there were only four residents at Presque Isle, and they were the woodcutters.

In the spring of 1840, on a later voyage of the steamer, CONSTELLATION, another writer, Frederick J. Starin, of New York, wrote that the vessel stopped off Thunder Bay Island on their voyage north but were unable to get any signal of life from the shore. This was around 7:00 p.m., Starin wrote. "There is a lighthouse on this island," he continued, "where there are a few acres cleared. The rest is one dense forest, and really a bleak, lonely and desolate place. About in the middle", he wrote, "I discovered a few miserable huts, probably abodes of fishermen, and I also saw several other small islands between Thunder Bay Island and the mainland, all heavily wooded."

As the result of a law passed in 1980, requiring the State of Michigan to set aside 5% of our Great Lakes bottomlands as recreational and historical areas, Thunder Bay in Lake Huron is now officially an "underwater preserve". A second such preserve has been designated for Pictured Rocks National Lakeshore near Munising in the Upper Peninsula.

The move, designed to protect the shipwrecks of Thunder Bay, actually began in the late 1960's when the state discovered that divers were stripping some of the bay's wrecks of historical items. In some instances, wrecks have been vandalized of their richly textured woods which were then used to make furniture. Today such looting is a crime punishable by a fine and a term in jail. Enforcement of the 1980 law is in the hands of the Michigan Department of Natural Resources.

Starting with Thunder Bay itself, and extending on northward past the snaggle-toothed rock reefs surrounding Middle Island, the shoals around False Presque Isle and the course changes at Presque Isle itself, this has been, and is yet, one of the more dangerous stretches of water on Lake Huron. A check of the following disaster statistics will show why some who have seen it at its best as well as at its worst, respectfully refer to it as "Lake Huron's wreck alley".

NAME OF SHIP	AREA OF SHIP	DATE
ADRIATIC, bark	Sank following collision	1863
AGATE, schr	Wrecked at Presque Isle	1856
ALBANY, stmr	Wrecked off Presque Isle	1853
ALLEGHANY, stmr	Wrecked on Summer Island	1896
ALLEN, E.B., schr	Lost in collision in Thunder Bay	1871
AMERICAN UNION, schr	Sank near Presque Isle	1894

NAME OF SHIP	AREA OF LOSS	DATE
ANDERSON, MAJOR, schr	Ashore off Middle Island (raised and later lost in Lake Michigan)	1863
AVON, prop	Foundered in gale off Presque Isle	1869
BALTIC, bge	Wrecked on Long Point	1872
BAY CITY, schr	Stranded off Alpena in Thunder Bay	1902
BEMIS, PHILO S., tug	Burned in Thunder Bay (salvaged, abandoned 1879)	1872
BERRIMAN, FRANCIS, bark	Collision off Alpena	1877
BIRCKHEAD, P.H., stmr	Burned at Alpena	1905
BISSEL, HARVEY, schr	In tow of stmr DAVID RUST, stranded at False Presque Isle, lumber cargo a total loss	1905
BLANCHARD, B., stmr	Wrecked on North Point near Thunder Bay Island	1904

HARVEY BISSELL...Schooner of 496 g.t., built in 1866 in Toledo, Ohio...in tow of DAVID RUST and stranded at False Presque Isle in 1905. Lumber cargo total loss.

NAME OF SHIP	AREA OF LOSS	DATE
BRAMAN, D.R., schr	Lost in storm off Black River	1870
BRIDGE, H.P., bark	Collision southeast of Thunder Bay Island	1869
BROOKLYN, schr	Wrecked near Alpena	1892
BRUCE, KATE L., schr	Lost off 40 Mile Point, all hands	1877
CANADA, prop	Sank near Rockport	1883
CHOCTAW, stmr	Collision off Presque Isle, 10 lives lost	1915
CONGRESS, prop	Stranded off Thunder Bay Island, (later wrecked)	1893
CORSICAN, schr	Lost in collision off Thunder Bay Island, 8 lives	1893
CZAR, schr	Wrecked and sank at False Presque Isle	1875
DARIEN, schr	Stranded at Presque Isle	1870
DAVIDSON, JAMES E., stmr	Foundered in Thunder Bay	1883

CHOCTAW...Propeller freighter of 1,574 g.t., built in Cleveland in 1892...lost in collision off Presque Isle in 1915...10 lost.

(Right) Purser Herbert McElroy and Captain Smith in front of the officers' quarters.

(Below) This window matches the ones behind McElroy and Smith above.

(Left) This 1912 photograph of the Titanic *shows the open forward A-Deck promenade which can also be seen (bottom) on the* Titanic *wreck.*

(Top) The cast-iron frame of a deck bench appears almost bronze in the light from Alvin.

(Above left) A toilet bowl lies next to a liquor bottle.

(Above right) A painted metal footboard from a first-class stateroom.

(Bottom) These wooden stairs may have taken third-class passengers from the Well Deck to the Poop Deck. Probably made of teak, the stairs are remarkably well preserved.

R.M.S. *Titanic*: Then and Now

Although the funnels are gone and the hull is broken, the wreck and debris field of the *Titanic* reveal fascinating glimpses of the great ship that was.

(Left) *The port-side Boat Deck of the* Titanic. *In the left foreground can be seen one of the "Sirocco" ventilation fans and its motor.*

(Above) *The fan and motor housings still rest in their original position after 74 years.*

(Above) A crab scuttles along the arm of a lifeboat davit that last saw use at 1:10 A.M. on April 15, 1912, as it lowered lifeboat No. 8.

(Opposite, top) The same davit can be seen holding lifeboat No. 8 behind the passenger at the rail.

(Opposite, bottom) The Titanic's *Welin davits were designed to carry 32 lifeboats, but they held only 16 — the number legally required by the British Board of Trade.*

The Debris Field

Like a silent underwater museum more than two miles down, debris lies scattered over the ocean floor near the *Titanic* wreck. Most of the debris is concentrated near the severed stern section which is 1,970 feet away from the more intact bow section.

(Left) This plain headboard from third class or the crew's quarters provides a strong contrast to the more elegant enameled footboard shown on the opposite page.

(Below) A grenadier fish and Alvin's arm inspect a third-class coffee cup bearing the White Star emblem.

NAME OF SHIP	AREA OF LOSS	DATE
DEMMER, EDWARD, stmr	Collision in Thunder Bay, sank	1923
EGAN, MARION, schr	Collision near Thunder Bay Island Light	1875
EGYPTIAN, prop	Burned 10 miles off Thunder Bay	1897
ELLEN, schr	Wrecked and sank	1856
ELVINA, schr	Foundered off Thunder Bay	1901
EMPIRE STATE, schr	Total loss in storm on Thunder Bay	1877
ENTERPRISE, stmr	Foundered in Thunder Bay (salvaged, made a barge)	1894
ETURIA, stmr	Collision off Presque Isle Light	1904
FISH, WM., brig	Wrecked at Devil River near Ossineke, S of Thunder Bay	1869
FLINT, OSCAR T., stmr	Burned off Thunder Bay	1909
FLORIDA, stmr	Collided with GEORGE ROBY off False Presque Isle and sank	1897
FRANKLIN, BEN, stmr	Wrecked in Thunder Bay	1853
FRANZ, W.C., stmr	Collision 8½ miles off Thunder Bay	1934
GALENA, stmr	Wrecked in Thunder Bay, all hands lost	1872
GARDNER, NELLIE, schr	Wrecked on Thunder Bay Island	1883
GILBERT, W.H., stmr	Collision off Thunder Bay Island	1914
GOLD HUNTER, schr	Wrecked off Thunder Bay Island, sank	1879
GOSHAWK, bge	Foundered in Thunder Bay	1920
GRECIAN, stmr	Sank in Thunder Bay	1906
GUENTHER, HERMAN, bge	Wrecked in Thunder Bay	1890
GUILLOTINE, schr	Lost near Middle Island	1881
GULNAIR, schr	Ashore and wrecked on Thunder Bay's North Point	1890

D.R. HANNA...Steamer involved in collision off Thunder Bay Island in 1919 and sunk. No casualties.

NAME OF SHIP	AREA OF LOSS	DATE
HANNA, D.R., stmr	Collision off Thunder Bay, sank	1919
HARVEST QUEEN, schr	Foundered off Presque Isle	1880
HARWICH, schr	Foundered above False Presque Isle, 7 lives lost	1858
HAVRE, schr	Sank off Middle Island	1845
HELEN C., stmr	Stranded in Thunder Bay, Alpena	1922
HOLMES, schr	Stranded on Middle Island Reef	1887
HORNER, MOLLY T., schr	Sank off Scarecrow Island	1906
IRONTON, schr	Collision near Presque Isle, 5 lives lost	1894
JOHNSON, J.T., schr	Wrecked on Thunder Bay Shoal	1902
JUPITER, schr	Lost south of Alpena	1901

NAME OF SHIP	AREA OF LOSS	DATE
KALIYUGA, stmr	Last seen off Presque Isle, 16 lives lost	1905
LaFARGE, FRANK, schr	Stranded and wrecked in Thunder Bay	1901
LARSEN, JULIA, schr	Stranded southeast of Thunder Bay Island	1912
MACKINAW, prop	Burned on Lake Huron near Black River	1890
McDERMOTT, bge	Blown ashore and wrecked 75 yards N of light	1902
MASON, NELLIE, schr	Burned between Presque Isle and Adams Point	1887
MAXWELL, WM., tug	Standed on Thunder Bay Reef	1908
MEEKER, LEWIS, schr	Foundered near Middle Island, all hands lost	1872
MERRICK, M.F., schr	Collision off Presque Isle in fog, 5 lives lost	1889
MIAMI, stmr	Burned in Thunder Bay	1924
MILDRED, tug	Foundered in heavy blow off Alpena	1872

KALIYUGA...Steamer of 1,941 g.t., built in St. Clair in 1887...last seen off Presque Isle, vanished with 16 casualties...1905.

MONOHANSETT...Propellor of 572 g.t., built in Gilbralter in 1872... sunk in storm on Thunder Bay just west of island in 1907.

NAME OF SHIP	AREA OF LOSS	DATE
MILLER, GRACE, *tug*	Sank in full gale in Thunder Bay	1875
MOFFAT, KATE, *tug*	Burned and sank at Presque Isle	1885
MOFFAT, GEO., *tug*	Lost in Presque Isle Bay	1864
MONOHANSETT, *stmr*	Foundered in Thunder Bay storm	1907
MONROVIA, *stmr*	Collision - sank off Thunder Bay Island	1959
MONTANA, *stmr*	Burned in Thunder Bay	1914
MONTANA, *schr*	Lost north of Middle Island, crew saved	1890
MORSE, FRED A., *schr*	Sank in collision southeast of Thunder Bay Island	1892
MORTON, J.D., *stmr*	Sank in Thunder Bay in storm	1853
MOWATT, JAMES, *schr*	Foundered off Alpena	1919

NAME OF SHIP	AREA OF LOSS	DATE
NAPLES, CITY OF, stmr	Wrecked off Presque Isle	1892
NEW ORLEANS, stmr	Foundered in Thunder Bay in heavy storm	1849
NEW YORK, stmr	Burned in Thunder Bay	1910
NOMAD, schr	Lost near Presque Isle	1871
NONPAREIL, schr	Stranded on Middle Island Reef, abandoned	1866
NORDMEER, stmr	On shoal north of Thunder Bay Island, still there	1966
NORMAN, prop	Sank in collision northeast of Middle Island, crew rescued by steamer SIKEN, 3 lives lost	1895
NORTH HAMPTON, brig	Foundered off Thunder Bay Island	1854
OCHS, JAY, tug	Foundered off Middle Island in gale winds	1905
OGARITA, schr	Burned off Thunder Bay Island, sank	1905
OHIO, prop	Collision north of Presque Isle, sank	1894
PALMER, E.B., schr	Foundered near Thunder Bay Island, crew saved	1892
PARKS, O.E., stmr	Foundered off Thunder Bay Island, sank	1929
PEWABIC, stmr	Collision in Thunder Bay, 125 lives lost	1865
PORTLAND, schr	Stranded at False Presque Isle	1867
PORTSMOUTH, stmr	Foundered and burned on Middle Island Reef	1867
RAAB, LUCY, schr	Struck Middle Island Reef, sank	1862
RAYNOR, ANNIE C., schr	Stranded on Middle Island Reef, broke up	1863
READ, W.P., stmr	Foundered off Alpena	1917
RED BOTTON, schr	Foundered on Middle Island Reef	1876

NAME OF SHIP	AREA OF LOSS	DATE
REPUBLIC, prop	Ashore and abandoned near Alpena	1898
RICE, JOHN, schr	Sank off Thunder Bay Island in heavy storm	1893
ROANOKE, schr	Sank in high winds near Alpena	1866
ROUNDS, W.H., schr	Stranded at Black River Reef in Thunder Bay in "BIG" storm	1905
RYAN, stmr	Total loss in heavy gale, Thunder Bay Island	1890
SHAMROCK, stmr	Foundered near Alpena in "BIG" storm	1905
SIMONS, WILLIAM, bge	Burned off Thunder Bay Island	1933
SNOW DROP, schr	Total wreck on North Point near Thunder Bay Island	1892
SPANGIER, K., schr	Foundered off Presque Isle	1860
STEVENS, J.H., schr	Burned offshore of Presque Isle	1927
STEVENS, W.H., schr	Stranded on Scarecrow Reef	1863
THEW, W.P., stmr	Sank in Thunder Bay storm, 3½ miles E. of Light	1909
THOUSAND ISLANDER, stmr	Sank near mouth of Thunder Bay	1928
TYPO, schr	Collision near Presque Isle, 9 lives lost	1899
VAN VALKENBURG, LUCINDA, schr	Collision north of Thunder Bay Island, sank	1887
VANDERBILT, schr	Burned near Sulphur Island	1882
VENUS, schr	Sank in Thunder Bay, all hands lost	1887
VIATOR, stmr	Collision and sank off Thunder Bay	1935
VICTORIA, prop	Driven ashore and wrecked near Kettle Point	1884
VIENNA, schr	Foundered north of Thunder Bay Island	1906

NAME OF SHIP	AREA OF LOSS	DATE
WARREN, WM. C., stmr	Stranded off Presque Isle	1947
WARNER, JOHN F., schr	Lost near Alpena	1890
WILSON, BELLE, stmr	Foundered in heavy weather in Thunder Bay	1888
WILSON, D.M., prop	Foundered northeast of Thunder Bay Island	1894
YOUNG, WM. A., schr	Foundered south of Middle Island	1911

SHIPWRECKS OF THE STRAITS OF MACKINAC

(A bonus that evolved as a result of our own interest in seeing a composite of all shipwrecks in this area)

The Multi-Storied Straits

Perhaps one of the most historic spots in all America, the Straits of Michilimackinac is the richest historical treasure house of the Great Lakes. Here, in a narrow band of blue water and on its shores as well as on one turtle-shaped island, vital chapters in the history of France and England and the United States were written. Here a teeming wilderness community of whites and Indians alike, lived and breathed and prospered...long before the white man had made inroads anywhere else in the midwest.

The white man is generally conceded to have first come here in 1630 and through his commercial efforts as well as lineage, made separate and distinct settlements at what we know today as St. Ignace, Mackinaw City and Mackinac Island. Michilimackinac was headquarters for Indian tribes from throughout the midwest. It was a fur-trading center; it was a fishing capital; it was a regular stop on the freight and passenger route of every vessel plying the upper Great Lakes. It was the key to all power, wielding control over the lakes and mid-America, and, as such, a valued prize for all nations competing for dominance in the New World. While three different countries claimed it at three different times in its history, Mackinac Island came back to the United States following the War of 1812 and was made a permanent part of our nation in 1815.

The island, or the "magic island" as some prefer to think of it, looks with detachment at the arching span of the great bridge that tied the two Peninsulas of Michigan together back in the 1950's. While the bridge brought a new flow of commerce and business across the four miles of water that had formerly made Michigan into two distinct parts, it did not deface the beauty, charm and historical ambience of the island. It is still, today, one of the most popular tourist and vacation sites in Michigan and the upper Great Lakes.

Looking out at the Straits as they funnel beneath the glittering roadway of the bridge, it doesn't take a lot of imagination to visualize some of those who've passed this way before.

The Indian, who was here when the white man first arrived in 1630 had known of the "magic straits" long, long before the first French explorer stumbled onto this intriguing crossroads of the New World. Even the Seminoles in the deep south and in the Florida everglades were aware of these big waters and the "narrows" that tied them together. Why they knew, and how, and for what, we to this day do not understand.

It's easy for the imagination to create panoramic pictures of the canoes of the primitive redman...the big bateau's of the Courier de Bois...the dashing voyageurs in their colorful trading canoes...perhaps even the many-oared, high-powered vessels of the Norse as they slid silently past. And, of course, the eye of the imagination cannot miss the black-frocked Jesuit Fathers with their crosses held high. There were so few of them to bring the warmth and love of their beliefs to a huge and hostile land. And think for just a moment; did the ancient Mound Builders pass this enroute to a new home? And the mysterious race that dug for copper hundreds upon hundreds of years ago on Isle Royale, did they also sweep through here as they fled the copperfields to seek asylum elsewhere? This was a part of upper Canada then as it is a part of our heritage now.

The Straits themselves, because they do connect Lake Huron and Lake Michigan with the different personalities and marine natures of the two lakes, have become known as one of the trickiest navigational areas of all the lakes. Also, due to the fact that *all* shipping going from one lake to another *must* pass through this narrow strait, the danger of collision is always at hand. As a result, and due to the merging currents, wind forces and general confinement of the area, we may have here a higher percentage of wrecks *per square mile* than anywhere else in the lakes. Add in the fact of the lack of navigational aids in the old days, plus an extremely poor communications and marine reporting system, and you will see why details on so many of these wrecks are as scanty as they are.

In researching material and data for this section of our "SHIPWRECKS OF LAKE HURON", we were quick to discover that we must define and detail the boundaries of that which we would accept as "Straits" area. As a result, and after careful study of the traffic patterns for the area, we determined that all shipping would have to be considered as being within the "Straits" area when traveling through the frequently tricky approach waters both east and west. This led us to ultimately include much of the South Channel, as well as the upper half of the North Channel and most of the waters east of Mackinac and Round Islands to Les Cheneaux and the general area of the Bois Blanc Light. To the west the area takes in Waugoschance, St. Helena Island and Shoal, White Shoal, Gray's Reef, Lansing Shoal and the treacherous approach waters surrounding

Ile aux Galet, better known to all sailormen as "Skillagalee". This then is our "Straits" area.

Again we remind you, this exclusive compilation of Lake Huron shipwrecks was done as a result of the author's lifetime residence on and interest in the Great Lakes, plus a quarter-of-a-century spent on the lakes as an accredited yachtsman. Our bibliography at the end of this volume indicates the scope of the research invested in the project between 1979 and 1983.

NAME OF SHIP	AREA OF LOSS	DATE
ABBELL, C.L., schr	Wrecked at Pt. Waugoschance	1861
ALASKA, schr	Wrecked on Bois Blanc	1884
ALBANY, schr	Wrecked in the Straits	1843
ALBEMARLE, schr	Foundered near Pt. Nipigon	1867
ALERT, brig	Wrecked at Waugoschance	1844
ALDRICH, WM., schr	Wrecked at Pt. Epoufette	1916
ANGLO-SAXON, bge	Sank in storm west of bridge area	1867
ARABIAN, brig	Foundered on Goose Island Shoal	1856
AVERY, WALDO, stmr	Burned 5 miles west of Mackinaw City (raised in 1894 as PHENIX, renamed LIBERTY, abandoned 1924)	1893
BARNEY, D.N., schr	Sank below 9 Mile Point	1868
BARNUM, W.H., stmr	Cut by ice 5 miles east of Mackinaw City, CRUSADER saved crew	1894
BEAVER, schr	Wrecked at 9 Mile Point	1890
BENTLEY, JAMES H.	Foundered east of Bois Blanc Island	1878
BONNIE DOON, schr	Wrecked off Bois Blanc	1867
BOSTON, CITY OF, stmr	Sank after collision (raised in 1870)	1868
BOURKE, MARY N., schr	Burned at Pine River north of Straits	1914

NAME OF SHIP	AREA OF LOSS	DATE
BRADLEY, ALVA, schr	Sank at Bois Blanc Island	1888
BRECK, JESSIE H., schr	Lost near 9 Mile Point	1890
BRIDGEWATER, schr	Wrecked at Waugoschance	1875
BURCHARDS, SARDIS, schr	Lost in Straits, position unknown	1879
BURNS, ROBERT, brig	Lost east of Bois Blanc (last full-rigged brig) 10 lives lost, (raised in 1872, lost in storm)	1869
BUTTS, L.C., #1., schr	Sank with coal cargo off Bois Blanc	1891
CALIFORNIA, stmr	Wrecked near St. Helena Island, 14 lives lost (rebuilt as EDW. PEASE, burned in 1904, Collingwood)	1887
CANISTEO, stmr	Wrecked in collision near Waugoschance	1880
CAYUGA, stmr	Collided with J.L. HURD in fog off Skillagalee, (sank, crew saved, engines salvaged)	1895
CEDARVILLE, stmr	Sank in Straits following collision with Norwegian freighter, TOPDALSFJORD, 10 of CEDARVILLE crew lost	1965
CHALLENGE, stmr	Exploded and burned near Cheboygan	1853
CHAMPION, schr	Stranded, west end of Bois Blanc Island (later salvaged)	1847
CIRCASSIAN, schr	Sank west of White Shoals	1860
CLARION, brig	Lost near Skillagalee	1860
CLARK, LUCY J., schr	Capsized north of Cross Village, Straits	1883
CLAY, HENRY, brig	Sank near Pt. Nipigon, Straits	1850
COLLINS, M.L., schr	Broke up and sank near Waugoschance	1903

CEDARVILLE...Steamer sunk in Straits of Mackinac after collison with a "saltie" in 1965.

NAME OF SHIP	AREA OF LOSS	DATE
COLONEL ELLSWORTH, schr	Sank 4 miles from Waugoschance after collision with schooner E. MAXWELL	1896
COLONEL CAMP, bark	Sank as result of collision in Straits	1856
COLONIAL, tug	Stranded and wrecked in Straits	1939
COLONIST, prop	Sank in Straits - position unknown	1869
COMMERCE, schr	Stranded and sank west side of Seul Choix Pt.	1895
CONDOR, schr	Sank at Skillagalee	1862
COWIE, WM., stmr	Burned at Cheboygan	1890
CROMWELL, OLIVER, prop	Sank in collision (raised 14 years later, 1871)	1857
CYGNET, tug	Burned off Cheboygan	1882
DAWN, schr	Sank in Straits following collision, 5 lives lost	1859
DEAN, JULIA, brig	Wrecked at Skillagalee	1855
DETROIT, schr	Foundered near Skillagalee with load of ore...(former MARY BATTLE)	1886

NAME OF SHIP	AREA OF LOSS	DATE
DOLPHIN, schr	Sank after collision at Waugoschance	1869
DOUSMAN, NANCY, schr	Foundered in Straits storm (raised)	1834
DREADNAUGHT, schr	Foundered and broke up at Seul Choix Pt.	1893
EDDY, NEWELL A., schr	Lost with all hands northwest of Spectacle Reef	1893
ELVA, bge	Burned and scuttled on island	1954
ENTERPRISE, scow	Broke up, sank in Straits	1861
FLIGHT, schr	Abandoned and burned, Bois Blanc	1865
FLOWER, R.P., stmr	Wrecked near Waugoschance	1892
FORESTER, schr	Foundered and raised the same year	1846
FREE STATE, stmr	Lost on Gray's Reef	1871
FULTON, E.A., schr	Foundered and raised the same year	1859
GENESEE CHIEF, schr	Sank off Cheboygan	1891
GEORGE E., tug	Burned at Cedarville, Les Cheneaux	1909
GERTRUDE, schr	Sunk by ice four miles north of Cheboygan	1868
GLAD TIDINGS, schr	Sank at 9 Mile Point	1898
GRANADA, schr	Stranded on Bois Blanc in 1873, salvaged and lost in Straits storm	1875
GRANGER, schr	Wrecked at Seul Choix Point in Straits	1896
GREEN BAY, CITY OF, schr	Foundered with 6 lives lost off Epoufette (may have been salvaged)	1887
HARRIET ANN, schr	Sank off 9 Mile Point	1859
HAYES, KATE, schr	Wrecked on Spectacle Reef	1856

NAME OF SHIP	AREA OF LOSS	DATE
HOWE, WM., schr	Sank near Seul Choix Pt. in Straits, 6 lives lost	1894
HUMPHREY, GEO. M., stmr	Sank following collision, (raised following year)	1943
HURD, JOSEPH, stmr	Collided with CAYUGA at Skillagalee - salvaged	1895
INDUSTRY, bge	Foundered off Lansing Shoal	1953
ISLAND QUEEN, schr	Sank at Waugoschance	1859
JESSIE, schr	Stranded on Bois Blanc	1890
JESSIE BRECK, schr	Foundered near 9 Mile Pt., 5 lives lost	1890
JOHNSON, HATTIE, schr	Stranded and sank off Goose Island Shoal	1868
JOHNSON, HENRY J., stmr	Sank in collision near Spectacle Reef	1902
JOHNSON, J.C., schr	Sank in storm behind St. Helena Island	1895
JURA, schr	Sank north of Cross Village	1911
KINGSFORD, THOS., schr	Sunk by ice near Waugoschance	1877
LADY WASHINGTON, stmr	Foundered near Seul Choix Point	1890
LaFRENIER, schr	Lost on Hog Island Shoal	1886
LAWRENCE, schr	Cut by ice and sank off St. Helena Island	1850
LEANDER, schr	Foundered and lost near Gros Cap	1857
LEE, OLIVER, bark	Wrecked above Old Mackinac Point	1859
LEVIATHAN, tug	Burned at Cheboygan	1891
LITTLE GEORGY, schr	Sank in Straits storm	1912
LUCKY, scow	Foundered at Cordwood Pt.	1957
LYONS, W.S., schr	Lost on White Shoals	1871
MAID OF THE MIST, schr	Wrecked at 9 Mile Point	1878

NAME OF SHIP	AREA OF LOSS	DATE
MAITLAND, bark	Sank as result of multiple collision north of Waugoschance	1871
MARIA, schr	Foundered in Straits storm	1841
MARQUETTE, schr	Lost in the Straits (later raised)	1870
MAROLD, oil screw	Exploded and burned, Simmons Reef	1937
MAUD, S., tug	Lost near Cheboygan	1888
McBRIER, FRED, stmr	Sank following collision	1890
MILLS, NELSON, stmr	Wrecked near Naubinway in Straits	1892
MILWAUKEE, stmr	Sank following collision with TIFFANY, 5 crew lost from TIFFANY	1859
MINNEAPOLIS, stmr	Sank between McGulpin's Pt. and Mackinaw City	1894
MONITOR, schr	Wrecked at Seul Choix Pt.	1883
MORTON, MINNIE, tug	Foundered off Bois Blanc	1881
NEVADA, stmr	Foundered and total loss near Bois Blanc, no lives lost	1890
NIGHTINGALE, schr	Sank near Spectacle Reef	1869
NORTHERN BELLE, schr	Sank after collision southwest of Skillagalee	1873
NORTHWEST, schr	Sank in storm near Big Stone Bay	1898
ODD FELLOW, brig	Lost in storm 3 miles from Mackinaw City	1854
OREGON, stmr	Lost in collision near Bois Blanc	1886
ORIENTAL, stmr	Lost at Skillagalee	1859
OSCODA, stmr	Lost on Pelkie Reef	1914
OUTHWAITE, J.H., stmr	Burned near Cheboygan off Pt. Nipigon	1905
PALMS, FRANCES, schr	Wrecked on Simmons Reef	1889

NAME OF SHIP	AREA OF LOSS	DATE
PATCHIN, A.D., stmr	Wrecked at Skillagalee	1853
PERSEVERANCE, schr	Sank in collision with GRAY EAGLE	1864
PESHTIGO, stmr	Foundered and broke up on Round Island	1908
PESHTIGO, bark	Collided with schooner ST. ANDREWS and sank near Cheboygan	1898
PLATT, JAS., schr	Foundered in Straits area (salvaged, sank)	1874
PRAIRIE STATE, stmr	Lost in Straits	1860
PULASKI, schr	Wrecked on Grosse Pt. north, northwest of Mackinac Island	1887
QUEEN CITY, schr	Wrecked on Hog Island Reef	1895
REMORA, stmr	Foundered in storm and burned at St. Ignace	1892
RIVERSIDE, schr	Wrecked on Garden Island Shoal, no lives lost	1887
ROANOKE, stmr	Burned off 14 Mile Point	1894
SANDUSKY, brig	Lost in Straits, 7 casualties	1856
SAWYER, J.D., schr	Ashore and broke up on Seul Choix Point	1893
SEA GULL, tug	Burned on Bois Blanc	1893
SHAW, J.E., schr	Foundered and lost off St. Helena Island	1856
SMITH, ANNA, stmr	Foundered near Cheboygan, 1 life lost	1889
SMITH, J.A., schr	Sank near Station Point Cabin	1887
SMITH, L.C., stmr	Foundered near 9 Mile Pt.	1905
SPRY, ELLIE, schr	Total loss, caught in a gale at Skillagalee, no lives lost	1887
ST. ANDREW, schr	Lost in collision with PESHTIGO near Cheboygan	1898
STALKER, M., schr	Collision, sank near area where CEDARVILLE lies	1886

NAME OF SHIP	AREA OF LOSS	DATE
STONE, WM., schr	Lost in Cecil Bay, Straits	1901
SUNRISE, bark	Sank near Bois Blanc Island	1871
TARRYNOT, schr	Sank off Bois Blanc	1860
TAYLOR, HELEN, stm. bge.	Foundered off St. Helena Island	1923
TIFFANY, J.H., schr	Sank in collision with MILWAUKEE, 5 lives lost	1859
TOLEDO, stmr	Wrecked in Straits - position unknown	1869
TOPSY, schr	Ashore and total wreck on St. Martins Point	1891
TORRENT, IDA M., stmr	Burned near Cross Village	1893
UGANDA, stmr	Sank near White Shoals	1913
UNCLE SAM, tug	Crushed in Straits ice and sank	1882
WALRUS, schr	Lost on Gray's Reef	1868

HELEN TAYLOR...Propellor of 82 g.t., built in 1894 in Grand Haven... foundered off St. Helena Island in Straits in 1923.

***UGANDA**...Propellor freighter of 2,054 g.t., built in West Bay City...lost in Straits area near Point Nipigon in 1913.*

***EBER WARD**...Propellor of 1,343 g.t., built in 1888 in West Bay City... foundered in the Straits of Mackinac in 1905 with five lives lost.*

NAME OF SHIP	AREA OF LOSS	DATE
WARD, EBER, stmr	Struck ice floe and sank, 5 lives lost near Cheboygan	1909
WARNER, CHAS. M., stmr	Lost near 9 Mile Point	1905
WELCOME, slp	Lost with all hands	1787
WELLINGTON, schr	Wrecked at Skillagalee	1867
WHITE FOAM, schr	Sank off Bois Blanc	1899
WHITE STAR, stmr	Burned at Cheboygan	1844
WHITE SWAN, stmr	Wrecked at Skillagalee	1956
WINSLOW, KATE, schr	Sank at Seul Choix Pt. (had sunk in 1881 at Meldrum Bay, Manitoulin and been raised)	1897
WINSLOW, RICHARD, schr	Sank at White Shoals	1898
WINSLOW, R.G., bark	Lost near Spectacle Reef	1867
WORTHINGTON, GEO., schr	Foundered near St. Helena, saved	1875
YANKEE BLADE, schr	Lost near Skillagalee, saved to sail again	1883

LAKE HURON... Where 40% of All Lake Ships Come to Die

NAME OF SHIP	AREA OF LOSS	DATE
ABBELL, C.L., schr	Wrecked at Pt. Waugoschance	1861
ABERCORN, stmr	Burned at Goderich	1904
ABIGAIL, schr	Sank in Georgian Bay (could be in North Channel)	1892
ACME, prop	Foundered on Lake Huron, 14 crew saved by RELIANCE	1893
ACONTIOUS, schr	Lost on Lake Huron	1887
ACORN, schr	Foundered near Harbor Beach	1876
ADA, schr	Sank at Collingwood in Georgian Bay	1859
ADAIN, schr	Wrecked and sank near Grindstone City	1890
ADAIR, schr	Wrecked on Charity Island in Saginaw Bay	1886
ADDIE B., schr	Stranded near Caseville in Saginaw Bay	1888
ADELE, tug	Burned at Drummond Island	1936
ADRIATIC, bark	Sank after collision on Lake Huron in Thunder Bay	1872
ADVANCE, stmr	Wrecked, Manitoulin Island in Georgian Bay	1927
AFRICA, prop	Sank on Lake Huron near Cove Island, 13 lives lost	1895
AFRICA, stmr	Burned at Owen Sound	1886
AGATE, schr	Wrecked at Presque Isle	1856
AGAWA, stmr	Stranded on Manitoulin Island	1927

AGAWA...Steamer stranded in December, 1927 on Manitoulin Island.

NAME OF SHIP	AREA OF LOSS	DATE
AGNES W., stmr	Stranded near Detour pounded to pieces	1918
AJAX, stmr	Burned in Saginaw Bay	1872
ALASKA, stmr	Sank near Tobermory in Georgian Bay	1910
ALASKA, schr	Wrecked on Bois Blanc	1884
ALBANY, stmr	Wrecked in Lake Huron off Presque Isle	1853
ALBANY, schr	Wrecked in the Straits	1843
ALBANY, stmr	Collision with PHILADELPHIA, 12 miles off Pte aux Barques with the loss of 24 lives	1893
ALBEMARIE, schr	Foundered in storm at the Straits	1867
ALBION, schr	Wrecked NE of Grindstone City, total loss	1887
ALDRICH, schr	Wrecked on Point Epoufett	1916

NAME OF SHIP	AREA OF LOSS	DATE
ALERT, brig	Wrecked at Waugoschance	1844
ALEXANDRIA, stmr	Burned at Little Current in Georgian Bay	1927
ALGOMA, stmr	Sank at Collingwood (formerly CITY OF TORONTO) ....Not to be confused with ALGOMA wrecked in 1885 in Superior with 38 lives lost.	1870
ALICE G., stmr tug	Wrecked near Tobermory	1927
ALLEGHANY, stmr	Wrecked on Summer Island, Thunder Bay	1896
ALLEN, E.B., schr	Lost in collision in Thunder Bay	1871
ALMERSON, THOS., schr	Foundered off Pt. Lookout, Saginaw Bay	1900
ALTAIR, schr	Wrecked near Chantry Island	1864
ALVA, D., tug	Burned in Beaverstone Bay, Georgian Bay	1914
ALVINA, schr	Foundered off Sturgeon Point	1900
AMARANTH, schr	Foundered near Port Huron (Later raised, became barge and wrecked at Port Huron in 1901)	1900
AMELIA, schr	Sank in Lake Huron off Goderich	1864
AMES, S.P., schr	Wrecked 2 miles ESE of Pte aux Barques Light	1895
AMERICAN UNION, schr	Sank near Presque Isle	1894
ANDERSON, MAJOR, schr	Ashore off Middle Island (raised and lost in Lake Michigan)	1863
ANDOVER, schr	Stranded on reef, Pte aux Barques	1861
ANGLO-SAXON, bge	Lost in the Straits of Mackinac	1887
ANNIE MARIA, schr	Foundered at Stony Island	1869
ANTELOPE, bge	Burned on the Saginaw River	1885

NAME OF SHIP	AREA OF LOSS	DATE
ARABIA, schr	Lost in Georgian Bay near Echo Island	1884
ARABIAN, brig	Foundered off Goose Island	1856
ARCTIC, schr	Lost in collision N-NE of Pte aux Barques	1895
ARCTIC, prop	Foundered south of Harbor Beach, total loss	1893
ARCTURAS, bge	Foundered in Saginaw Bay	1888
ARGUS, stmr	Sank 25 miles west of Kincardine, 25 lives lost	1913
ARIEL, schr	Wrecked near Collingwood	1870
ARK, bge	Foundered in Lake Huron, 4 lives lost	1866
ARK, schr	Stranded near Grindstone City	1887
ARMSTRONG, C.W., tug	Burned on Saginaw River in Bay City	1870
ASHTON, MAGGIE, schr	Wrecked north of Grindstone City	1899

ARGUS...Steamer sunk off Inverhuron in Lake Huron in 1913's "big storm"...all hands lost.

NAME OF SHIP	AREA OF LOSS	DATE
ASIA, stmr	Sank in Georgian Bay storm with 123 lives lost	1882
ATHABASCA, stmr	Foundered near Lonely Island in Georgian Bay	1910
ATHENIAN, schr	Wrecked off Oscoda.	1880
ATHENS, stmr bge	Broke up and foundered off Southhampton, Ont.	1917
ATLANTIC, stm bge	Lost off docks at Harrisville	1895
ATLANTIC, stmr	Burned in Georgian Bay in lee of Pancake Islands	1903
ATWATER, S.T., schr	Wrecked on Manitoulin Island	1895
AUDUBON, JOHN, brig	Sank after collision below Pte aux Barques	1854
AUSTIN, schr	Sank off Port Austin in Saginaw Bay, 7 lives lost	1883
AVERY, WALDO, prop	Burned 5 miles west of Mackinaw City, raised in '94	1893
AVON, prop	Foundered off Presque Isle	1869
AZOV, schr	Foundered at Pte aux Barques, capsized and drifted to Chantry Island	1911
B.C. & CO., bge	Sank at Saginaw	1870
BADGER STATE, stmr	Burned and sank with 15 lives lost	1909
BAHAMA, schr	Foundered in heavy gale off Alpena, total loss	1895
BALTIC, prop	Burned at Collingwood (formerly the FRANCIS SMITH)	1896
BALTIC, barge	Wrecked on Long Point in Thunder Bay	1872
BALTIMORE, stmr	Sank off Oscoda with 14 lives lost	1901
BARNEY, D.N., schr	Collision and sank in the Straits near 9 mile point	1868
BARNUM, W.H., stmr	Cut by ice 2 miles east of Mackinaw City, ship total loss but crew rescued by CRUSADER	1894

NAME OF SHIP	AREA OF LOSS	DATE
BARTLETT, tug	Burned in Saginaw River at Bay City	1884
BAVARIAN, schr	Stranded 1 mile south of Cape Smith, Manitoulin, crew of 8 saved by Indians	1898
BAY CITY, schr	Stranded off Alpena in Thunder Bay	1902
BEAVER, schr	Wrecked at 9 Mile Pt.	1861
BECKER, B.H., tug	Sank off Greenbush	1937
BEHM, LENA, schr	Burned off Port Hope - total loss	1900
BELL, DANIEL, stmr	Burned in Saginaw Bay near Bay City	1859
BELLE, stmr	Foundered in Georgian Bay	1852
BEMIS, PHILO S., tug	Burned in Thunder Bay, 1872 - repaired & abandoned	1879
BEN HUR, schr	Sank near Port Huron following collision	1890
BENTLEY, JOHN, schr	Sank, storm in Georgian Bay near Cabbage Head	1886
BENTLEY, JAMES H., schr	Foundered east of Bois Blanc Island	1878
BERLIN, schr	Total wreck near Grindstone City, 4 lives lost	1877
BERRIMAN, FRANCIS, bark	Collision off Alpena in Thunder Bay	1877
BERTHIER, stmr	Burned on lake in storm	1914
BETSCHY, JACOB, stmr	Wrecked in Saginaw Bay on Port Austin Reef	1879
BIELMAN, C.F., prop	Built in Bay City in 1892, Wheeler Yard, now the breakwater at Great Duck Island	
BIRCKHEAD, P.H., stmr	Burned at Alpena	1905
BIRDIE, schr	Sank off Hammond Bay	1892
BISHOP, H.B., schr	Foundered in Georgian Bay	1852

C.F. BIELMAN...Built at Wheeler yard to 2,056 g.t., in Bay City, Michigan in 1892...now a breakwater at Great Duck Island.

NAME OF SHIP	AREA OF LOSS	DATE
BISSEL, HARVEY, schr	In tow of stmr DAVID RUST, stranded at False Presque Isle - lumber cargo a total loss	1905
BLAKE, J.W., schr	Wrecked off Sturgeon Point	1855
BLAKE, E.R., schr	Burned on the lake	1898
BLANCHARD, B.E., stmr	Wrecked on North Point near Thunder Bay Island	1904
BLISH, E.D., schr	Sank in Huron with all hands lost	1864
BOLIVIAN, schr	Stranded at Sand Beach	1877
BOLTON, SAMUEL, schr	Broke in two on rocks in fog - no casualties (near Richmondville)	1893
BOND, O.M., schr	Sank at Sand Beach	1879
BONNIE BOAT, stmr	Stranded and broke up near Kincardine	1869

NAME OF SHIP	AREA OF LOSS	DATE
BONNIE DOON, slp	Burned at Meldrum Bay	1880
BONNIE DOON, schr	Wrecked at the Straits near Bois Blanc Island	1867
BONNIE MAGGIE, stmr	Wrecked at Kincardine	1868
BOODY, A., schr	Stranded on Pte aux Barques Reef in Saginaw Bay	1887
BOSTON, CITY OF, stmr	Sank after collision in Straits (raised 1870)	1868
BOURKE, MARY N., schr	Burned at Pine River, St. Ignace	1914
BOWMAN, C.M.	Wrecked near Vail's Point, Georgian Bay	1915
BRADLEY, ALVA, schr	Sank at Bois Blanc Island	1888
BRAINARD, KATE, schr	Foundered off Kincardine	1871
BRAMAN, D.R., schr	Lost in offshore storm near Black River	1870
BRANT, scow	Sank in Lake storm	1859
BRECK, MARY L., schr	Wrecked near Tobermory	1900
BRECK, JESSIE H., schr	Lost near 9 Mile Point	1890
BREDEN, JOHN, schr	Foundered off Lexington with 3 lives lost	1899
BRENTON, schr	Lost on Lake Huron	1899
BRIDGE, H.P., bark	Collision southeast of Thunder Bay Island	1869
BRIDGEWATER, schr	Wrecked at Waugoschance	1875
BRITTAIN, R.C., stmr	Burned at Sarnia	1912
BRODER, ELIZABETH, schr	Wrecked - Manitoulin Island	18--
BROOKLYN, schr	Wrecked near Alpena in Thunder Bay	1892
BROTHERS, schr	Wrecked near Goderich, crushed by ice field	1869
BROWN, WILLIE, tug	Burned on the river in East Saginaw	1889
BRUCE, KATE L., schr	Lost off 40 Mile Point with all hands	1877

NAME OF SHIP	AREA OF LOSS	DATE
BRUCE MINES, stmr	Foundered off Cape Hurd, all hands lost	1854
BRUNO, stmr	Sank south of Cockburn in a collision, total loss, accident occurred on Magnetic Reef	1890
BUCEPHELUS, prop	Foundered in Saginaw Bay with 10 lives lost	1854
BUCEPHELUS, schr	Sank in Saginaw Bay	1879
BUCKEYE, bge	Burned and sank in Georgian Bay	1885
BUCKINGHAM, schr	Sank in Saginaw Bay	1870
BUCKLEY, EDWARD, stmr	Burned on Manitoulin, Georgian Bay	1929
BUFFALO, CITY OF, bark	Wrecked on the end of piers at Sand Beach	1875
BURLINGTON, prop	Built in Bay City, burned at Meldrum Bay	1895
BURCHARDS, SARDIS, schr	Wrecked on Lake Huron in the Straits	1879
BURNS, ROBERT, brig	Foundered east of Bois Blanc Island in the Straits (the last full-rigged brig) raised 1872 but lost	1869
BUTTS, L.C., No. 1.	Total loss in South Channel off Bois Blanc	1891
CAHOON, THOS. H., schr	Sank at Innes Island, North Channel	1913
CALIFORNIA, stmr	Wrecked at St. Helena Island, 14 lives (salvaged 1889 as Edw. F. Pease, burned 1904, Collingwood)	1887
CAMBRIA, stmr	Wrecked and sank	1897
CAMPBELL, P.M., tug	Burned at Manitoulin	1898
CANADA, stmr	Burned at Port Huron	1892
CANADA, prop	Sank near Rockport	1883
CANADIAN, schr	Foundered near Clara Island in the Whalesback	1880

NAME OF SHIP	AREA OF LOSS	DATE
CANESTEO, stmr	Burned near Port Huron	1920
CANISTEO, stmr	Wrecked on Waugoschance in the Straits	1880
CARDINGTON, M.D., schr	Wrecked in Saginaw Bay off Au Sable Point	1873
CARIBOU, stmr	Scuttled near Sault Ste Marie	1947
CARKIN, W.S., tug	Sank - position unknown	1887
CAROLINE, schr	Capsized and sank off Duck Islands	1832
CARRIN, F., stmr	Foundered in lake storm	1912
CARRUTHERS, JAS., stmr	Wrecked and sank near Kincardine, 18 lives lost	1913
CARTER, J.S., schr	Wrecked at Carter Rock in Mississagi Straits	1890
CARTIER, JACQUES, stmr	Wrecked near Goderich	1878
CASCADEN, schr	Foundered near Tobermory	1871
CASTALIA, brig	Sank in Georgian Bay storm	1871
CAVALIER, schr	Foundered off Chantry Island	1906
CAYUGA, prop	Sank in collision at Skillagalee with J.L. HURD, crew saved	1895
CEDARVILLE, stmr	Sank after collision in Straits 2 miles E of city	1965
CELTIC, schr	Wrecked on southeast point of Cockburn Island, all hands lost	1902
CHALLENGE, stmr	Burned at Cheboygan	1853
CHALLENGE, tug	Burned at East Saginaw in the river	1880
CHAMBERLAIN, stmr	Wrecked on Georgian Bay	1901
CHAMPION, schr	Stranded at west end of Bois Blanc Island (later salvaged)	1847
CHATTANOOGA, schr	Built by Davison, Bay City (now part of breakwater at Great Duck Island)	

NAME OF SHIP	AREA OF LOSS	DATE
CHEBOYGAN, CITY OF, schr	Wrecked near Detour	1880
CHECOTAH, schr	Foundered off Port Sanilac	1906
CHENANGO, prop	Lost without a trace	1891
CHEROKEE, stmr	Lost with 2 barges off Saginaw Point	1913
CHERUB, ycht	Burned and sank in Saginaw River at Bay City	1974
CHICKAMAUGA, schr	Foundered off Harbor Beach (sister ship to the CHATTANOOGA)	1919
CHIEF, GENESEE, schr	Foundered off Cheboygan	1891
CHINA, schr	Sank in Georgian Bay near Cape Hurd	1883
CHOCTAW, stmr	Collision off Presque Isle with 10 lives lost	1915
CINCINNATI, stmr	Stranded and ashore at Forestville	1854
CITY QUEEN, tug	Lost in Georgian Bay	1924
CIRCASSIAN, schr	Sank in the Straits	1860
CLARION, brig	Lost at Skillagalee	1860
CLARK, LUCY J., schr	Capsized at Cross Village	1883
CLARK, JAMES, tug	Burned at Owen Sound	1896
CLARK, S.C., stmr	Burned off Port Sanilac	1893
CLARKE, J.C., stmr	Burned near Sarnia	1905
CLAY, HENRY, brig	Sank in the Straits of Mackinac near Pt. Mipigon	1850
CLAYTON, bark	Collision and sank	1868
CLAYTON BELLE, schr	Sank in collision off Lexington, 4 lives lost	1882
CLEMENT, N.P., stmr	Scuttled in Georgian Bay	1968
CLEVELAND, prop	Burned off Charity Islands in Saginaw Bay	1880
CLEVELAND, CITY OF, stmr	Burned in Lake Huron off Perserverance Island	1901

NAME OF SHIP	AREA OF LOSS	DATE
CLIFTON, stmr	Foundered north of Oscoda, all 27 hands lost	1924
COAST GUARD CUTTER 40'	Sank at Gravelly Shoal	1967
COBURN, R.G., prop	Foundered near Pte aux Barques, Saginaw Bay with 32 lives lost	1871
COCHRANE, TOM, stmr	Wrecked on Sturgeon Point	1862
COE, S.S., tug	Burned and sank near Port Austin	1876
COHEN, E., schr	Wrecked on Port Hope Reef - total loss	1890
COLFAX, schr	Sank near Detour	1870
COLONEL BRACKETT, stmr	Total loss in northeast gale near Harbor Beach	1890
COLONEL CAMP, bark	Sank in Straits collision	1856
COLONEL CARRY, bark	Foundered off Goderich	1854
COLONEL DAVIS, tug	Burned at Port Huron	1889
COLONEL ELLSWORTH, schr	Total loss in collision at Waugoschance	1896
COLONIAL, tug	Stranded at the Straits	1939
COLONIST, prop	Wrecked in the Straits	1869
COLLINGWOOD, schr	Burned at Byng Inlet, Georgian Bay	1878
COLLINGWOOD, CITY OF	Burned at the wharf at Collingwood, Georgian Bay	1905
COLLINS, M.L., schr	Stranded and broken up near Waugoschance	1903
COLUMBIA, stmr	Lost in storm, unable to determine cause or position	1866
COMAN, L.D., schr	Wrecked at Pte aux Barques	1865
COMMERCE, schr	Stranded and sank west side of Seul Choix Pt.	1899
COMMERCE, schr	Lost in big storm that swept the Lakes	1905
CONDOR, schr	Lost near Skillagalee	1862

NAME OF SHIP	AREA OF LOSS	DATE
CONGER, OMAR D., stmr	Exploded and burned at Port Huron	1922
CONGRESS, prop	Stranded off Thunder Bay Island 1868, later wrecked	1893
CONSUELO, stmr	Foundered north of Harbor Beach	1887
CONSUELO, schr	Wrecked off Marble Head, North Channel (salvaged)	1885
CONWAY, J.L., schr	Sank in Lake Huron, 5 lives lost	1886
CORAL, stmr	Foundered on Lake Huron	1887
CORSAIR, schr	Foundered off Sturgeon Pt.	1872
CORSICAN, schr	Lost following collision off Thunder Bay Island, 8 lives lost	1893
COWIE, WM., prop	Burned at Cheboygan	1890
CRANAGE, THOM., stmr	Wrecked on Watcher's Reef, Georgian Bay, total loss	1911
CREAM CITY, stmr	Wrecked on Wheeler's Reef, False Detour, with 2 schooners in tow	1918
CREOLE, tug	Burned at Wye River in Georgian	1905
CRISPIN, brig	Stranded at Pte aux Barques	1853
CROMWELL, schr	Sank off Harbor Beach	1888
CUMBERLAND, brig	Wrecked in Lake Huron (salvaged and re-wrecked at Milwaukee)	1856
CROMWELL, OLIVER, prop	Sank in Straits collision (raised in 1871)	1857
CURLEW, schr	Foundered in river at Saginaw	1890
CUYAHOGA, prop	Sank near Sarnia	1866
CUYLER, GLEN, schr	Lost in the "big" storm of the year	1905
CYCLONE, bge	Lost at Alabaster in Saginaw Bay (the former steamer PITTSBURGH)	1885

GLEN CUYLER...*Schooner of 49 g.t., built in 1859 in Pultneyville and lost on Lake Huron in storm of 1905.*

NAME OF SHIP	AREA OF LOSS	DATE
CYGNET, tug	Burned at Cheboygan	1882
CYGNET, bge	Exploded and burned in Saginaw Bay	1875
CZAR, schr	Wrecked and sank at False Presque Isle	1875
DAISY, stmr	Destroyed by fire at Port Hope	1895
DALTON, PETER, tug	Sank in Lake Huron	1896
DANA, GEORGE, bge	Wrecked in Lake Huron	1876
DANAY, LILLIE, schr	Wrecked near Kincardine	1865
DANCEY, LILY, schr	Foundered near Port Elgin	1856
DARIEN, schr	Stranded at Presque Isle	1870
DAUNTLESS, schr	Total wreck at Martin's Reef	1870
DAUNTLESS, schr	Sank in Sarnia Bay	1889
DAUNTLESS, schr	Wrecked near Fort Gratiot	1895

NAME OF SHIP	AREA OF LOSS	DATE
DAVIDSON, FRED, tug	Sank at Point au Baril, Georgian Bay	1916
DAVIDSON, JAS. E., prop	Foundered in Thunder Bay	1883
DAVIS, GEORGE, schr	Ashore in Saginaw Bay	1901
DAVIS, J.H., schr	Swamped and sank in northern squall, total loss	1893
DAWN, schr	Sank in Straits following collision, 5 lives lost	1859
DEAN, JULIA, brig	Wrecked at Skillagalee	1855
DEER, tug	Burned off AuGres, Saginaw Bay	1908
DELAWARE, prop	Wrecked in Hammond Bay	1887
DEMMER, EDW., stmr	Collision in Thunder Bay - sank	1923
DESPATCH, tug	Wrecked on Pte aux Barques	1871
DETROIT, schr	Former Mary Battle, lost near Skillagalee (ore load)	1886
DETROIT, II, stmr	Sank after collision with Brig NUCLEUS, Saginaw Bay	1854
DETROIT, CITY OF, prop	Sank in Saginaw Bay, all 20 hands lost	1863
DICKINSON, GEO. B., tug	Lost in collision near Bay City, Saginaw Bay	1886
DOBBINS, ANNA, tug	Foundered in Saginaw Bay near the Charity Islands	1886
DOLPHIN, schr	Sank after collision near Waugoschance	1869
DOLPHIN, schr	Foundered near Harbor Beach	1887
DORMER, bge	Sank in Saginaw River near Crow Island	1940
DORR, E.P., tug	Collision in Saginaw Bay and sank	1856
DOUGLASS, stmr	Dismantled on Lake Huron	1921
DOUSMAN, NANCY, schr	Foundered in the Straits of Mackinac, (salvaged)	1834

NAME OF SHIP	AREA OF LOSS	DATE
DREADNAUGHT, schr	Collision in Saginaw Bay near AuGres (salvaged) stranded & broken up on Seul Choix Pt., 1893.	1886
DREW, GEO. C., schr	Wrecked at Charity Island in Saginaw Bay	1866
DUDLEY, dredge	Foundered off Au Sable Point in Saginaw Bay	1934
DUFFERIN, LADY, schr	Wrecked on Dufferin Point in Georgian Bay	1886
DUNBAR, GEORGE, stmr	Sank from storm damage with 7 lives lost	1902
DUNCAN, JOHN, stmr	Wrecked and sank off Harrisville	1905
DUNCAN, MAGGIE, schr	Wrecked off docks at Harrisville	1895
DUNCAN CITY, schr	Lost in North Channel in the Georgian	1888
DUNDERBURG, schr	Collision 6 miles off Harbor Beach	1868
DUNLAP, GEO. L., stmr	Sank from ice damage 14 miles from Bay City	1880
EAGLE, tug	Burned in Saginaw Bay	1869
EAST SAGINAW, prop	Foundered near Harrisville	1875
EASTNOR, stmr	Burned at Wiarton	1933
ECLIPSE, schr	Disappeared on Lake Huron with no visible reason	1883
ECLIPSE, stmr	Sank with all hands lost	1874
EDDY, NEWELL A., schr	Foundered at the Straits with all hands lost	1893
EGAN, MARION, schr	Collision near Thunder Bay Island Light	1875
EGYPTIAN, prop	Burned 10 miles off Thunder Bay	1897
ELITE, tug	Burned at Jennie Island in Georgian Bay	1933

ESCANABA...Steamer lost in 1894 in Lake Huron...not to be confused with ESCANABA, the propeller built in 1881 at Gibralter.

NAME OF SHIP	AREA OF LOSS	DATE
ELIZABETH, schr	Foundered near Detour - victim of "big storm"	1882
ELLEN, schr	Wrecked and sank in Thunder Bay	1856
ELVA, bge	Scuttled and burned in Straits near Mackinac Island	1954
ELVINA, schr	Foundered off Thunder Bay	1901
ELY, GEO. H., bge	Sank near Detour - swamped by storm	1882
EMERALD, bge	Sank in Saginaw River, total loss	1880
EMERY, H.A., schr	Foundered near Harbor Beach	1899
EMEU, schr	Sank near Grindstone City, total loss	1888
EMILY, schr	Total wreck in Georgian Bay	1858

NAME OF SHIP	AREA OF LOSS	DATE
EMMA, tug	Burned in Georgian Bay near Sister Rock Beacon	1912
EMMA, schr	Lost near Blue Point	1869
EMPIRE STATE, schr	Total loss in storm on Thunder Bay	1877
ENTERPRISE, prop	Lost in storm near Green Island with many lost	1894
ENTERPRISE, scow	Broke up and sank in Straits of Mackinaw	1861
ENTERPRISE, schr	Foundered near Barrie Island in Georgian Bay	1903
ENTERPRISE, stmr	Foundered off Pte aux Barques (raised)	1883
ENTERPRISE, stmr	Foundered in Thunder Bay (salvaged and made a barge)	1894
ERIE, stmr	Ice collision off Port Huron and sank	1842
ERIE BELLE, tug	Sank after boiler explosion at Kincardine, 4 lost	1883
ESCANABA, stmr	Position unknown	1894
ESPERANCE, schr	Sank in Saginaw Bay (one of the first locally built)	1842
ESPERANZA, slp	Burned at Cape Croker in Georgian Bay	1907
ESSEX, stmr	Burned at Sarnia	1884
ETRURIA, stmr	Collision off Presque Isle Light, total loss	1904
EUGENE, schr	Wrecked in storm at Port Austin Reef in Saginaw Bay	1867
EUREKA, schr	Foundered off Kincardine	1901
EUREKA, slp	Totally wrecked off Au Sable	1869
EVA, tug	Burned on Lindsay Bank, 3/4 miles N of Drummond Island	1881
EVENING STAR, stmr	Sank in Saginaw Bay near Gravelly Shoal	1841

NAME OF SHIP	AREA OF LOSS	DATE
EVENING STAR, schr	Foundered at Goderich	1894
EVERETT, A.E., prop	Foundered north of Pte aux Barques in Saginaw Bay ice	1895
EXCELSIOR, schr	Burned on the Saginaw River	1869
EXILE, schr	Foundered off Sturgeon Point	1916
EXPERIMENT, bge	Lost near Lexington	1866
EXPLORER, schr	Sank in Stokes Bay...with 5 lives lost	1883
FAME, bark	Foundered in lake storm off Goderich	1854
FARRAR, C.M., tug	Lost in explosion off Port Huron	1873
FASHION, stmr	Lost in Lake Huron off Bayfield, Ont.	1856
FASSETT, THEO. S., schr	South of Harbor Beach (later salvaged)	1898
FAY, JOSEPH, stmr	Foundered near Rogers City	1905
FERGUSON, bge	Sank at East Tawas	1886
FERRIS, B.F., stmr	Burned at Caseville	1891
FILLMORE, MILLARD, schr	Sank at Rogers City	1891
FISH, WM., brig	Wrecked at Ossineke south of Thunder Bay	1869
FLANDE, prop	Collision and sank	1897
FLETCHER, KATE, tug	Burned on river in Saginaw	1877
FLIGHT, schr	Abandoned on Bois Blanc Island	1865
FLINT, OSCAR T., stmr	Burned off Thunder Bay	1909
FLORIDA, stmr	Collision with Geo. W. Roby off False Presque Isle and sank	1897
FLOWERS, R.P., stmr	Wrecked near Waugoschance	1892
FOOTE, COMM., schr	Collision in Lake Huron and sank	1867
FORBES, CHRISTIAN, tug	Burned on river near Bay City	1895

NAME OF SHIP	AREA OF LOSS	DATE
FORD, J.C., stmr	Burned near Detour	1924
FOREST, schr	Foundered off Kincardine	1857
FOREST CITY, stmr	Wrecked at Bears Rump near Tobermory	1904
FORESTER, schr	Foundered at the Straits and raised	1846
FORESTER, schr	Lost off Port Sanilac	1898
FORTUNE, schr	Disappeared on Lake Huron	1864
FORWARDER, schr	Lost near Kincardine	1864
FOSTER, A.M., prop	Foundered at Pte aux Barques following collision	1888
FOSTORIA, schr	Wrecked in storm near Detour	1874
FRANCE, bark	Foundered off Goderich	1854
FRANKLIN, BEN, stmr	Wrecked in Thunder Bay	1853
FRANZ, W.C., stmr	Collision 8½ miles off Thunder Bay	1934
FREE STATE, prop	Wrecked near Gray's Reef in the Straits area	1871
FREEDOM, schr	Capsized 15 miles N. of Fort Gratiot, 3 lives	1844
FRONTIER CITY, brig	Lost near Kincardine - wrecked and total loss	1871
FULTON, E.A., schr	Foundered in the Straits of Mackinac, (salvaged)	1859
FULTON, ROBERT, stmr	Wrecked at Sturgeon Point	1844
GALATEA, schr	Collision near Harbor Beach	1924
GALE, S.E., brig	Sank following collision with schooner TELEGRAPH	1850
GALENA, stmr	Wrecked in Thunder Bay, all hands lost	1872
GAME, schr	Lost in Georgian Bay near Collingwood	1871
GARDEN CITY, stmr	Wrecked near Detour on Martin's Reef	1854

THEODORE S. FASSETT...Schooner of 548 g.t., built in Marine City. sunk south of Harbor Beach in 1898.

NAME OF SHIP	AREA OF LOSS	DATE
GARDEN CITY, stmr	Burned 4 miles from Bay City	1903
GARDNER, NELLIE, schr	Wrecked on Thunder Bay Island	1883
GARIBALDI, schr	Foundered in Georgian Bay with 4 lives lost	1865
GARY D., tug	Burned near Strawberry Island, North Channel	1958
GEORGE E., tug	Burned at Cedarville, Les Cheneaux Islands	1909
GENERAL, tug	Burned at Detour	1920
GENESEE CHIEF, schr	Sank off Cheboygan	1891
GEORGIAN, stmr	Foundered near Owen Sound in Georgian Bay	1884
GERMANIC, stmr	Burned at Collingwood in in Georgian Bay	1917
GERTRUDE, schr	Sunk by ice 4 miles west of Mackinaw City	1868
GETWORK, stmr	Burned at Collingwood in Georgian Bay	1917
GIANT, tug	Sank in Saginaw River	1894
GIDLEY, J.C., tug	Burned near Meldrum Bay	1909
GILBERT, W.H., stmr	Collision off Thunder Bay Island	1914
GILPHIE, stmr	Burned at Lion's Head in Georgian Bay	1909
GLAD TIDINGS, schr	Foundered in Hammond Bay near 9 Mile Pt.	1898
GLADSTONE, schr	Lost near Port Huron	1883
GLENORCHY, stmr	Collision 10 miles ESE of Harbor Beach	1924
GLENSTRIVEN, stmr	Wrecked on Georgian Bay	1923
GLOBE, stmr	Burned in Saginaw Bay (raised and made a barge)	1863
GLOBE, MV	Foundered in Saginaw Bay	1954
GOLDEN FISHER	Burned off Cape Hurd	1943

NAME OF SHIP	AREA OF LOSS	DATE
GOLD HUNTER, schr	Wrecked in Thunder Bay	1879
GOLDEN WEST, schr	Foundered in Georgian Bay near Snake Island	1884
GOLIATH,* prop	Boiler explosion off Lexington and sank, 18 lost	1847
GOODELL, N.P., schr	Foundered in Lake Huron on Yankee Reef in westerly gale, crew reached Canada	1891

* Sometimes listed as GOLIAH

GOODNOW, WM., tug	Collision off Lexington and sank	1869
GOODREAU, stmr	Stranded in storm on Lake Huron, S. shore of Lyal Island	1917
GOODYEAR, FRANK, stmr	Collision with 18 lives lost, hit J.B. WOOD, sank	1910

GLENORCHY...Steamer of 2,465 g.t., lost in collision with another vessel near Harbor Beach in 1924.

NAME OF SHIP	AREA OF LOSS	DATE
GORE, stmr	Dismantled (vessel from which Gore Bay is assumed to have gotten its name)	1880
GOSHAWK, lbr bge	Foundered north of Tawas Point	1920
GOULD, E.F., stmr	Wrecked near Oscoda	1898
GOVERNOR SMITH, stmr	Collision off Pte aux Barques, Saginaw Bay	1906
GRAHAM, bark	Capsized in Lake Huron	1872
GRAHAM, JENNIE, bark	Foundered near Duck Islands, now a reef	1880
GRAHAM, GEO. A., stmr	Foundered off Manitoulin Island	1917
GRANADA, schr	Stranded on Bois Blanc Island in the Straits	1873
GRAND RAPIDS, CITY OF, stmr	Burned near Tobermory in Georgian Bay	1907
GRANGER, schr	Wrecked at Seul Choix Point in Straits	1896
GRANSNER, G.J., stmr	Sank following collision in fog	1911
GRECIAN, stmr	Sank in Thunder Bay	1906
GREEN BAY, CITY OF, stmr	Burned in Saginaw Bay	1909
GREENE, T.M., stmr	Lost in Lake Huron	1894
GREEN, C.R., tug	Foundered off Detour	1915
GRENADA, schr	Lost in Straits (may be same boat stranded in 1873)	1875
GRIFFON, gunboat	Lost in Lake Huron (perhaps near Mississagi)	1679
GROVER, CHRIS, schr	Stranded near Au Sable (sank in Superior in 1899)	1880
GUENTHER, HERMAN, bge	Wrecked in Thunder Bay	1890
GUILLOTINE, schr	Lost near Middle Island	1881
GULNAIR, schr	Ashore and wrecked on Thunder Bay's North Point	1890

T.M. GREENE...Propeller freighter of 523 g.t., built in Gibralter in 1887...lost in Lake in 1894.

NAME OF SHIP	AREA OF LOSS	DATE
HACKETT, H.J., stmr	Burned on the lake	1905
HACKETT, ALICE, schr	Lost near Fitzwilliam Island in Georgian Bay	1828
HALE, O.J., bge	Sank near Port Sanilac	1890
HALE, E.B., prop	Foundered in Saginaw Bay, crew saved by NEBRASKA	1897
HALL, S.C., stm bge	Sank at Sand Beach	1884
HAMONIC, stmr	Burned at Pt. Edward	1945
HANDY, AUGUSTUS	Stranded on Spectacle Reef, sunk	1861
HANNA, D.R., stmr	Collision off Thunder Bay and sank	1919
HANNA, HOWARD, stmr	Foundered on Port Austin Reef, Saginaw Bay (raised)	1913
HARRIET ANN, schr	Sank off 9 Mile Pt.	1859
HARRISON, J.C., schr	Lost in Lake Huron at Oscoda	1885

NAME OF SHIP	AREA OF LOSS	DATE
HART, ASA, schr	Foundered in Lake Huron, year of first big four-day storm	1869
HART, HARRIET A., stmr	Burned near Detour, total loss	1905
HARVEST QUEEN, schr	Foundered off Presque Isle	1880
HARWICH, schr	Foundered above False Presque Isle, 7 lives lost	1858
HATTIE, MARY, schr	Lost near Harbor Beach	1888
HAVRE, schr	Sank off Middle Island	1845
HAWGOOD, A.D., stmr	Foundered on reef near Harbor Beach	1911
HAYES, KATE, schr	Wrecked on Spectacle Reef	1856
HECTOR, schr	Foundered in Saginaw Bay	1903
HELEN C., stmr	Stranded in Thunder Bay, Alpena	1922
HELEN B., tug	Lost near Gull Island, Georgian Bay	1936
HERCULES, bge	Lost in Lake Huron	1870
HERCULES, dredge	Sank south of Oscoda, opposite Tawas Light	1932
HERCULES, schr	Sank in Michael's Bay, Manitoulin Island	1892
HIBBARD, W.B., schr	Stranded near Southhampton, total loss	1867
HIBOU, stmr	Sank 4 miles out of Owen Sound near Squaw Point, 7 lost	1936
HINCKLEY, CHAS., bge	Foundered in Lake Huron	1886
HOIGHT, KITTIE, schr	Burned in Lake Huron	1899
HOLLAND, schr	Broke up on Wheeler's Reef, False Detour	1918
HOLLAND, JOSEPH, schr	Lost in Lake Huron, 3 lives lost	1870
HOLLISTER, JOHN, stmr	Foundered in Lake Huron	18 --

NAME OF SHIP	AREA OF LOSS	DATE
HOLMES, schr	Stranded on Middle Island Reef	1887
HOLT, GEO. W., schr	Stranded on Port Austin Reef in Saginaw Bay	1880
HOPE, schr	Lost in Georgian Bay	1858
HOPE, schr	Wrecked in lake squall	1867
HOPE, slp	Foundered near St. Joseph's Island	1804
HORNER, MOLLY T., schr	Sank offshore of Scarecrow Island, Thunder Bay	1906
HORTON, ANNA, prop	Lost near Kincardine, no casualties	1871
HOTCHKISS, LEWIS, prop	Foundered west of Goderich	1891
HOWE, WM., schr	Sank near Seul Choix	1894
HUBBARD, HENRY, schr	Capsized in Lake Huron, all hands lost	1845
HUMPHREY, GEO. M., stmr	Straits collision (raised in 1944)	1943
HUNTER, schr	Lost at Harrisville, Lake Huron	1872
HUNTER, ELVIRA, schr	Foundered in Lake Huron	1895
HUNTER SAVIDGE, schr	Lost off Pte aux Barques with 5 lives lost	1899
HURD, JOSEPH, stmr	Collided with CAYUGA at Skillagalee, (later raised and salvaged)	1895
HURON, stmr	Foundered off Port Austin Reef, Saginaw Bay	1861
HUTCHINSON, EMMA, schr	Wrecked and sank off Harrisville	1880
HYDE, H., scow	Lost in Lake Huron off Point aux Barques	1883
HYDRUS, stmr	Foundered near Lexington, 28 lives lost BIG storm	1913
IDA & MARY, scow	Lost at Sturgeon Point	1872

NAME OF SHIP	AREA OF LOSS	DATE
ILLINOIS, bge	Foundered in Lake Huron (was first "steamer through Sault Ship Canal in '55	1869
IMPERIAL, schr	Lost in Georgian Bay	1889
INDIA, stmr	Burned and sank near W. Mary Island, North Channel	1928
INDUSTRY, bge	Foundered on Lansing Shoal in Straits area	1953
INTEROCEAN, stmr	Burned at Sarnia	1892
IRON CHIEF, stmr	Foundered off Pte aux Barques, Saginaw Bay	1904
IRONTON, schr	Collision near Presque Isle with 5 lives lost	1894
IROQUOIS, tug	Burned in McBean Channel, North Channel	1906
IROQUOIS, stmr	Wrecked and burned at Spanish Mills, North Channel	1908
IROQUOIS, bark	Lost on Lake Huron. (May be one built by French in 1760 and returned to trade after War of 1812)	1864
ISABELLA, schr	Wrecked on Lake	1864
ISHPEMING, schr	Wrecked north of Sturgeon Point	1903
ISLAND QUEEN, schr	At Straits of Mackinac	1859
ISLET PRINCE	Burned at Chantry Island	1938
ITASCA, stmr	Collided with Parks Foster and sank off Lexington	1895
JACKSON, ANDREW, schr	Foundered at Pte aux Barques in Saginaw Bay	1901
JAMAICA, schr	Capsized after collision	1872
JENKS, J.M., stmr	Stranded and wrecked north of Midland	1913
JESSIE, schr	Stranded at Bois Blanc Island	1890
JESSIE BRECK, schr	Foundered near 9 Mile Point, 5 lives lost	1890

NAME OF SHIP	AREA OF LOSS	DATE
JEWETT, JOHN, schr	Lost in Hammond Bay, Lake Huron	1898
JOHNSON, LEVI, tug	Explosion in Saginaw River with 4 lives lost	1867
JOHNSON, C.H., schr	Sank off St. Helena Island, no lives lost	1895
JOHNSON, HATTIE, schr	Sank in Hammond's Bay in gale	1868
JOHNSON, HENRY, stmr	Collision off Spectacle Reef and sank	1902
JOHNSON, J.T., schr	Wrecked on Thunder Bay Shoal	1902
JOHNSON, WILLARD, schr	Foundered at Pte aux Barques	1865
JOLLY INEZ, stmr	Sank off Saddlebag Reef, near Detour	1927
JONAS, schr	Sank following collision in Georgian Bay	1898
JONES, B.B., tug	Boiler explosion at Port Huron, 7 lives lost	1871
JONES, J.H., stmr	Foundered near Lion's Head in Georgian, 26 lost	1906
JONES, J.V., schr	Foundered in Lake Huron, year of "big storm"	1905
JOSEPH, bge	Lost near Caseville, Saginaw Bay	1885
JOYLAND, stmr	Aground near Manitoulin, burned by Burnt Island	1926
JULIA, schr	Foundered near Harbor Beach	1896
JULIET, stmr	Sank following collision off Port Huron	1911
JUPITER, schr	Lost south of Alpena	1901
JURA, schr	Sank near Cross Village	1911
KALIYUGA, stmr	Last seen off Presque Isle, 16 lives lost	1905
KALOOLAH, stmr	Lost off Goderich	1862

NAME OF SHIP	AREA OF LOSS	DATE
KATAHDIN, prop	Wrecked in "big storm"	1905
KATHADIN, schr	Lost in Lake Huron	1862
KEEWEENAH, schr	Sank in Neebish Rapids	1889
KEEPSAKE, bge	Foundered in Lake Huron, year of "big storm"	1905
KELLER, WILLIE, schr	Collision off Au Sable Point in Saginaw Bay	1888
KENOSHA, prop	Burned off Sarnia	1864
KEOSAGAS, stmr ycht	Burned at the mouth of Saginaw River	1916
KEYSTONE STATE, stmr	Foundered in Saginaw Bay with 33 lives lost	1861
KIDD, JOSEPHINE, prop	Burned in Georgian Bay	1882
KIMBALL, S.H., schr	Sank in a collision with Steamer G. Stone, northwest of Pte aux Barques, crew saved	1895
KINCARDINE, prop	Lost on French River, Georgian Bay	1888
KING, CHAS. A., schr	Foundered near Pte aux Barques, crew saved	1895
KING, FOREST, schr	Lost in Georgian Bay, sank due to storm violence	1869
KING, JAMES, schr	Wrecked near Tobermory	1901
KINGSFORD, THOS., schr	Sunk by ice near Waugoschance	1877
LACKAWANA, stmr	Sank following collision with unknown vessel	1909
LADY FRANKLIN, schr	Wrecked in Hammond Bay	1895
LADY OF THE LAKE, stmr	Collision at Christian Island, Georgian Bay	1911
LADY WASHINGTON, schr	Foundered near Sturgeon Point	1828
LADY WASHINGTON, stmr	Foundered at Seul Choix Pt., Straits	1890

NAME OF SHIP	AREA OF LOSS	DATE
LaFARGE, FRANK, schr	Stranded and wrecked at Thunder Bay	1901
LaFRENIER, schr	Lost on Hog Island Shoal	1886
LAMBERT, R.T., schr	Stranded near Caseville, Saginaw Bay	1873
LANDBO, stmr	Sank near Oscoda	1919
LANCASTER, bge	Lost in Bayfield Sound, North Channel	1907
LANGELL BOYS, stmr	Burned southeast of Au Sable Point, Saginaw Bay	1931
LANGELL, SIMON, prop	Burned at Sarnia	1936
La PETITE, schr	Lost on Lake Huron	1871
LARSEN, JULIA, schr	Stranded southeast of Thunder Bay Island	1912
LAWRENCE, schr	Cut by ice and sank near St. Helena Island	1850
LEANDER, schr	Foundered in the Straits	1857
LEE, FREDERICK, tug	Foundered northeast of Pte aux Barques, 5 lives lost	1936
LEE, JOHN, SR., stmr	Burned at Pt. McNicol, Georgian Bay	1913
LEE, LAURA, tug	Burned at Meldrum Bay	1929
LEE, OLIVER, bark	Stranded, Straits of Mackinac (former LONDON)	1859
LEHIGH, stmr	Sank following collision in heavy weather	1914
LELAND, prop	Burned in Lake Huron	1888
LEVIATHAN, tug	Burned at Cheboygan	1891
LEWIS, SAM, prop	Lost at Cape Croker, Georgian Bay	1871
LIKEN, CHAS. W., stmr	Burned on the river in Bay City	1905
LIKEN, J.C., prop	Foundered in Hammond Bay, gale winds, total loss	1890

LINDEN...Propeller freighter of 894 g.t., built in 1895 in Port Huron... burned in Tawas Bay in 1913.

NAME OF SHIP	AREA OF LOSS	DATE
LINCOLN, stmr	Lost in Lake Huron near Fishing Islands	1871
LINCOLN, A., schr	Stranded at Au Sable	1872
LINDEN, stmr	Burned in Tawas Bay	1923
LINN, WM. R., stmr	Foundered north of Point Edward	1918
LISGAR, schr	Wrecked near Cove Island, Georgian Bay	1899
LITTLE GEORGY, schr	Foundered in the Straits of Mackinac	1912
LITTLE NELL, stmr	Exploded on the Saginaw River at Saginaw	1862
LIVELY, schr	Foundered near Harbor Beach	1878
LODI, schr	Sank after collision with CHATAUQUE near Sturgeon Point	1842
LONDON, CITY OF, stmr	Burned in Collins Inlet, Georgian Bay	1875

NAME OF SHIP	AREA OF LOSS	DATE
LONG, JOHN, tug	Burned at Meldrum Bay	1900
LOOMIS, EDW., stmr	Wrecked near Harrisville	1934
LOWELL, brig	Lost near Cove Island, Georgian Bay	1871
LOWELL, prop	Burned off Port Huron	1893
LUCKNOW, stmr	Burned at Midland, Georgian Bay	1935
LUCKPORT, tug	Burned at Midland, Georgian Bay	1936
LUCKY, scow	Stranded at Cordwood Point near Cheboygan	1957
LUFF, SOPHIA L., schr	Wrecked in Georgian Bay	1892
LUMMIS, B.R.	Foundered in Lake Huron, all hands lost but one	1872
LURLINE, stmr yht	Wrecked off Goderich	1907
LYDIA, schr	Lost on Lake Huron, victim of "big storm"	1905
LYONS, KATE, schr	Disappeared on Lake Huron, year of "big" storm	1905
LYONS, W.S. schr	Lost on White Shoals	1871
MACKINAW, prop	Burned on Lake Huron near Black River	1890
MADDEN, LIZZIE, stmr	Burned off Point Lookout, Saginaw Bay	1907
MAGIC, schr	Sank in Saginaw Bay (later raised)	1861
MAGGIE, scow	Lost in Lake Huron, ashore near Goderich, total	1871
MAGNETTEWAN, prop	Ashore (wrecked on shoal near Byng Inlet)	1896
MAID OF THE MIST, schr	Lost on 9 Mile Pt.	1878
MAIME, scow	Foundered near Pte aux Barques	1858
MAINE, prop	Burned off Port Huron	1880
MAITLAND, bark	Collision at the Straits (Golden Harvest & Mears)	1871

NAME OF SHIP	AREA OF LOSS	DATE
MAITLAND, ALEX, stmr	Burned at Port Huron	1924
MAJESTIC, stmr	Burned at Sarnia	1915
MALAKOFF, schr	Foundered in Lake Huron off Goderich	1857
MANISOO, stmr	Sank in Georgian Bay, 16 lives lost	1928
MANISTIQUE, stmr	Scuttled in Lake Huron	1933
MANITOULIN, stmr	Burned near Manitowaning, 30 lives lost	1882
MAPLEDAWN, stmr	Foundered at Christian Island, Georgian Bay	1924
MARGRETTA, tug	Burned off Grindstone City	1907
MARIA, scow	Lost at 9 Mile Point	1875
MARIA, schr	Foundered at the Straits	1841
MARIA ANN, schr	Total ship loss off Kincardine, 4 lives lost, 2 saved	1901
MARINE CITY, schr	Foundered off Goderich, 4 lives lost	1901
MARINE CITY, stmr	Burned off Alcona, 8 to 10 lives lost	1880
MAROLD, prop	Exploded and burned on Simmon's Reef	1937
MARQUIS, schr	Lost near Harbor Beach	1892
MARQUETTE, bge	Burned in Essexville	1924
MARQUETTE, schr	Lost in the Straits (later raised)	1870
MARTIN, C.C., tug	Foundered at Key Harbor, Georgian Bay	1911
MARTIN, J.B., schr	Lost in Lake Huron, all hands lost	1869
MARTIN, JOHN, schr	Lost in collision off Fort Gratiot	1900
MARTIN, JOHN, tug	Foundered in Georgian Bay	1890
MARY ANN, tug	Lost in Georgian Bay, 2 lives lost	1883

NAME OF SHIP	AREA OF LOSS	DATE
MARY & LUCY, schr	Wrecked on Chantry Island	1879
MARY, schr	Ashore and wrecked near Goderich	1846
MASON, JANE, schr	Stranded off Oscoda	1889
MASON, L.G., stmr	Burned in Saginaw River near Lafayette bridge	1890
MASON, NELLIE, schr	Burned between Presque Isle and Adams Point	1887
MASSILON, schr	Foundered above Pte aux Barques, Saginaw Bay	1876
MATILDA, bge	Lost in storm on Lake Huron	1886
MATOA, stmr	Lost on Port Austin Reef, Saginaw Bay (raised)	1913
MATTAWAN, stmr	Stranded south of Forestville	1888
MAUD, S., tug	Lost near Cheboygan	1888
MAUTENEE, schr	Foundered in Lake Huron (year of the "BIG" blow)	1905
MAXWELL, schr	Lost near Goderich	1886
MAXWELL, WM., tug	Stranded on Thunder Bay Reef	1908
MAYFLOWER, brig	Foundered in Lake Huron squall	1867
MAYFLOWER, stmr	Burned at Penetanguishene	1900
MAY, VERBENA, tug	Wrecked near Stokes Bay	1896
MAYO, NELLIE, tug	Burned near Saginaw	1870
MAYS, NELLIE, tug	Burned on the Saginaw River near Saginaw	1887
MAZEPPA, stmr	Wrecked off the Saugeen - total loss	1856
McBRIER, A.J., stmr	Burned on Georgian Bay	1907
McBRIER, FRED, stmr	Collision at the Straits	1890
McCLELLAN, schr	Foundered in Lake Huron with 4 lives lost	1883

MARY McGREGOR...Propeller freighter built in Grand Haven of 711 g.t., wrecked on Magnetic Reefs off Cockburn Island in 1920.

NAME OF SHIP	AREA OF LOSS	DATE
McDERMOTT, bge	Blown ashore and wrecked 75 yds. N. of Thunder Bay Light	1902
McDONALD, CHAS. A., tug	Burned on the river in Saginaw	1894
McDONALD, J.H., tug	Burned at Southhampton	1934
McGEAN, JOHN A., stmr	Lost near Goderich, Lake Huron, 28 lives lost	1913
McGREGOR, MARY A., stmr	Cockburn's Magnetic Reef, burned with no lives lost	1920
McGRUDER, J.H., schr	Wrecked at Harrisville, broke up with total loss	1895
McKERRAL, P.R., stmr	Burned at Collingwood, Georgian Bay	1878
McLEAN, ANDREW A., tug	Foundered southeast of Tawas in Saginaw Bay	1916
McLEOD, JANE, schr	Lost near Parry Sound	1890

NAME OF SHIP	AREA OF LOSS	DATE
McPHEE, BELLE, schr	Sank off Collingwood	1876
McRAE, WM. F., tug	Sank in Lake Huron	1895
McVIE, MARY, prop	Foundered at Walkers Point, Manitoulin	1878
MEAFORD, CITY OF, stmr	Burned at Collingwood, Georgian Bay	1919
MEEKER, LEWIS, schr	Foundered near Middle Island, all hands lost	1872
MEISEL, C.A., bge	Stranded near Lakeport	1871
MELBOURNE, stmr	Sank in river at Bay City	1918
MERCER, schr	Lost in Lake Huron, year of the four-day storm	1869
MERCHANT, schr	Wrecked at Pte aux Barques, 5 lives lost	1849
MERRICK, M.F., schr	Collision off Presque Isle, 5 lives lost	1889
MERRILL, JOHN B., slp	Foundered off Drummond Island and totaled, no lives lost	1893
MESSENGER, stmr	Burned off Rogers City	1890
METAMORA, tug	Burned near Parry Sound	1890
METEOR, stmr	Lost on Spanish River, North Channel	1883
METROPOLE, stmr	Sank north of Port Austin	1903
MIAMI, stmr	Burned in Thunder Bay, no casualties	1924
MICHIGAN, brig	Wrecked on reef at Pte aux Barques	1870
MICHIGAN, stmr	Foundered at Hope Island, Georgian Bay	1943
MICHIPICOTEN, prop	Burned at Cook's Dock, Bayfield Sound (also listed as E.K. ROBERTS)	1927
MIDLAND CITY, stmr	Burned at Midland, Georgian Bay	1955
MIDLAND, CITY OF, stmr	Burned at Collingwood	1916

NAME OF SHIP	AREA OF LOSS	DATE
MIDNIGHT, schr	Total loss in southeast gale, crew saved	1889
MILDRED, tug	Foundered off Alpena in Thunder Bay	1872
MILLER, ALBERT, prop	Burned off Oscoda	1882
MILLER, E.M., tug	Burned on river in Saginaw	1874
MILLER, GRACE, tug	Sank in Thunder Bay	1875
MILLER, JANE, stmr	Wrecked at Colpoy Bay, 30 lives lost	1881
MILLIS, M.I., tug	Lost in collision off Sand Beach	1873
MILLS, NELSON, stmr	Wrecked off Naubinway in Straits	1892
MILTON, JOE, tug	Burned in Georgian Bay	1904
MILWAUKEE, stmr	Collision at Straits, schooner TIFFANY, 5 lives lost from TIFFANY	1859
MILWAUKEE, CITY OF, schr	Foundered in Lake Huron above Sanilac	1875
MINCH, CHAS. P., schr	Lost in Georgian Bay near Cove Island	1898
MINER, J.T., schr	Total loss at Caseville	1877
MINER, JULIA, schr	Lost east of Pte aux Barques	1894
MINNEAPOLIS, prop	Foundered and sank in Straits near McGulpin's Pt.	1894
MINNEDOSA, schr	Foundered off Harbor Beach, all 9 lives lost	1905
MINNESOTA, schr	Lost in Lake Huron, year of the "BIG" storm	1905
MINOR, JOHN, schr	Lost at Pte aux Barques in Saginaw Bay	1902
MIRANDA, schr	Wrecked at Port Austin	1871
MOCKING BIRD, tug	Burned near Cheboygan	1890
MOFFAT, GEO., tug	Lost in Presque Isle Bay	1864
MOFFATT, FRANK, tug	Lost in Lake collision near Port Huron	1873

NAME OF SHIP	AREA OF LOSS	DATE
MOFFATT, KATE, tug	Burned and sank at Presque Isle	1885
MOHAWK, stmr	Lost in Lake Huron, (former Canadian Revenue Cutter) at Pte aux Barques	1870
MOHEGAN, brig	Foundered in Lake Huron, at Pte aux Barques	1870
MOLLIE, scow	Sank off Sarnia	1881
MONA, schr	Lost at Pte aux Barques Reef, all lives lost	1887
MONITOR, schr	Total wreck at Seul Choix in Straits	1883
MONOHANSETT, stmr	Foundered in Thunder Bay storm and burned	1907
MONROVIA, stmr	Collision off Thunder Bay Island, sank 13 miles east	1959
MONSON, schr	Foundered near Port Hope	1851
MONTANA, stmr	Burned in Thunder Bay	1914
MONTANA, schr	Lost north of Middle Island, crew saved	1890
MONTEAGLE, stmr	Burned on St. Mary's River	1909
MONTEZUMA, brig	Lost in collision above Pte aux Barques	1871
MONTICELLO, schr	Lost near Port Austin, Saginaw Bay	1904
MONTGOMERY, stmr	Burned at Point Edward	1878
MONTMORENCY, schr	Wrecked at Charity Island	1901
MOORE, W.A., tug	Sank in Saginaw Bay	1871
MORRELL, DANIEL, stmr	Foundered north of Port Austin...28 lives lost	1966
MORSE, FRED A., schr	Sank in collision southeast of Thunder Bay Island	1892
MORRIS, schr	Foundered near Port Huron	1887
MORRISON, A.H., stmr	Foundered off Christian Island, Georgian Bay	1902

NAME OF SHIP	AREA OF LOSS	DATE
MORTON, J.D., stmr	Sank in Thunder Bay	1853
MORTON, MINNIE, tug	Foundered off Bois Blanc Island	1881
MORTON, SYLVIA, schr	Lost in Lake Huron	1887
MOSS, A.H., schr	Lost in Lake Huron	1887
MOUNTAINEER, schr	Stranded in Georgian Bay, total loss	1864
MOWATT, JAMES, schr	Foundered off Alpena in Thunder Bay	1919
MUNSON, ISSAC, schr	Stranded near Caseville in Saginaw Bay	1888
MYSTERY, stmr	Burned in Georgian Bay	1911
MYSTIC, tug	Foundered at Cockburn Island, North Channel	1878
NAIAD, stmr	Sank off Pte aux Barques (later raised)	1911
NANCY, H.M.S., schr	Burned on Nancy Island, Georgian Bay (now Museum)	1814
NAPLES, CITY OF, stmr	Wrecked off Presque Isle	1892
NAPOLEAN, stmr	Foundered off Saugeen Peninsula	1857
NARRAGANSET, schr	Lost in Hammond Bay	1872
NARRAGANSETT, schr	Foundered near Port Sanilac	1901
NASHUA, prop	Lost near Bayfield in NW "gale", 14 lives lost	1892
NEECHEE, schr	Wrecked on Russell Island near Tobermory	1863
NEILSEN, EMMA L., schr	Collision, sank 11 miles N. of Pte aux Barques	1911
NEILSON, schr	Lost in Lake Huron	1905
NELL, ELSIE, tug	Burned at Drummond Island	1936
NEMESIS, schr	Lost near Bayfield	1883
NEPTUNE, stmr	Burned on river in East Saginaw	1874

NAME OF SHIP	AREA OF LOSS	DATE
NESHOTO, schr	Foundered near Sturgeon Pt., 5 lives lost	1872
NESSON, N.J., stmr	Foundered near Meaford (salvaged, sank in Erie '29)	1919
NEVADA, stmr	Foundered, total loss near Bois Blanc (no life lost)	1890
NEWARK, schr	Lost in Lake storm	1864
NEWAYGO, stmr	Lost in Lake Huron near Tobermory	1903
NEW HAMPSHIRE, schr	Foundered in Lake near Sturgeon Point	1885
NEW ORLEANS, stmr	Foundered in Thunder Bay (former VERMILION)	1849
NEW YORK, stmr	Foundered off Harbor Beach	1876
NEW YORK, stmr	Burned in Thunder Bay	1910
NICHOLAS, stmr	Abandoned in Lake Huron	1913
NIGHTINGALE, schr	Stranded on Spectacle Reef, victim of 4-day blow	1869
NINA, schr	Sank in storm at Harrisville	1875
NOMAD, schr	Lost near Presque Isle	1871
NONPAREIL, schr	Stranded on Middle Island Reef, abandoned	1866
NORDMEER, stmr	Lost north of Thunder Bay	1966
NORMAN, prop	Sank in collision NE of Middle Island, 3 lives lost crew rescued by steamer SIKEN	1895
NORRIS, schr	Foundered in Lake Huron	1887
NORTH HAMPTON, brig	Foundered off Thunder Bay Island near Alpena	1854
NORTH STAR, stmr	Lost off Sanilac in collision	1908
NORTH WIND, stmr	Sank northeast of Clapperton Island, south of Crocker Island	1926
NORTHERN BELL, stmr	Destroyed by fire on Lake	1899

NAME OF SHIP	AREA OF LOSS	DATE
NORTHERN BELLE, prop	Burned at Byng Inlet	1857
NORTHERN BELLE, schr	Wrecked in collision southwest of Skillagalee	1873
NORTHERN LIGHT, bge	Burned at Harrisville docks	1881
NORTHERN QUEEN, stmr	Wrecked at Kettle Point	1913
NORTHERN STAR	Sank in collision with ONTONAGON	1856
NORTHERNER, stmr	Collision at Port Huron, 12 lives lost, 130 saved	1856
NORTHWEST, ycht	Lost off Harbor Beach	1904
NORTHWEST, schr	Wrecked and sank in Straits near Big Stone Bay	1898
OCEAN, brig	Lost in Lake Huron	1865
OCEAN, schr	Foundered at Tawas in Saginaw Bay	1873
OCHS, JAY, tug	Foundered off Middle Island, gale winds and seas	1905
ODD FELLOW, brig	Wrecked at the Straits of Mackinaw 3 miles from city	1854
OGARITA, schr	Burned off Thunder Bay Island	1905
OGDEN, WM. B., schr	Sank off Goderich, raised and sank again at Oscoda	1881
OHIO, prop	Lost in collision north of Presque Isle	1894
OKENZA, tug	Burned at Wiarton	1878
OLD CONCORD, bge	Foundered in Georgian Bay off Lion's Head	1888
OLGA, schr	Lost in Lake Huron near Goderich	1905
OLIVER LEE, bark	Sank above Old Mackinac Point	1859
ONAWA, prop	Burned at Cheboygan	1954
ONTARIO, tug	Burned off Port Huron	1883
OPHIR, tug	Burned at Parry Sound	1919

NAME OF SHIP	AREA OF LOSS	DATE
OREGON, stmr	Collision near Bois Blanc Island	1886
OREGON, stmr	Wrecked and burned near Thessalon, North Channel	1908
ORIENTAL, prop	Lost at Skillagalee with two wrecking pumps	1859
ORION, schr	Foundered at Pte aux Barques Reef (later sank near St. Joseph, 1861)	1856
ORONTES, bge	Wrecked and sank at Pt. Edward	1883
OSBORNE, J.M., prop	Sank after collision near Owen Sound	1884
OSCELOA, prop	Foundered near Grindstone City	1888
OSCODA, stmr	Wrecked on Pelkie Reef	1914
OSPREY, tug	Burned in Georgian Bay	1895

OREGON...Propeller of 974 g.t., built in 1892 in West Bay City...lost in Lake Huron in 1905 with all hands.

NAME OF SHIP	AREA OF LOSS	DATE
OSSIFRAGE, stmr	Foundered off Sturgeon Point	1900
OSWEGATCHIE, prop	Lost near Sturgeon Point plus 2 or 3 barges	1891
OTTAWA, schr	Sank after collision off Sarnia	1875
OUTHWAITE, J.H., stmr	Burned near Cheboygan off Pt. Nipigon	1905
OWEN, tug	Burned at Tawas	1921
OWEN, JOHN, stmr	Burned at Port Huron	1860
OWEN SOUND, CITY OF, prop	Wrecked at Clapperton Island, raised and later lost in Lake Huron as the SATURN	1887
OXFORD, stmr	Wrecked in Fishing Islands	1855
PACIFIC, prop	Burned at Collingwood docks, towed out and sunk	1898
PALESTINE, schr	Ashore in Lake Huron (later salvaged)	1848
PALMER, E.B., schr	Foundered near Thunder Bay Island, crew saved	1892
PALMETTO, schr	Sank in Lake Huron collision	1865
PALMS, FRANCES, schr	Foundered in the Straits on Simmons Reef	1889
PARAGON, schr	Total wreck at Sarnia	1868
PARISIEN	Lost near Goderich	1890
PARANA, bark	Foundered on Saginaw Bay	1863
PARKS, O.E., stmr	Foundered off Thunder Bay Island	1929
PARRY SOUND, CITY OF, stmr	Burned at Collingwood	1900
PATCHIN, A.D., stmr	Wrecked at Skillagalee in the Straits	1853
PATTER, H.C., stmr	Total loss in heavy gale in Saginaw Bay	1891
PEARL, schr	Wrecked on East Sister Reef, Georgian Bay	1855
PEASE, EDWARD, stmr	Burned at Collingwood (former California wrecked in Straits in 1887)	1904

NAME OF SHIP	AREA OF LOSS	DATE
PECK, *bge*	Foundered near Harbor Beach	1885
PEG, *tug*	Wrecked on Cockburn Island	1878
PENFIELD, J.P., *schr*	Lost in Lake Huron	1870
PENINSULA, *stmr*	Foundered in Lake Huron	1853
PERRY, COMM., *cutter*	Wrecked at Sturgeon Point	1877
PERSEVERANCE, *schr*	Sank in Straits, collision with GRAY EAGLE	1864
PESHTIGO, *stmr*	Foundered, aground & wrecked on Round Island	1908
PESHTIGO, *bark*	Lost in collision with schooner St. Andrews	1898
PERSIAN, *schr*	Collision, sank off 40 mile Pt., 10 lives lost	1868
PEWABIC, *prop*	Collision in Thunder Bay, 125 lives lost	1865
PFOHL, *stmr*	Burned near Goderich	1903
PHILADELPHIA, *prop*	Collision with ALBANY in fog, 24 lives lost	1893
PHILIP, *tug*	Burned at Detour	1933
PIERCE, MARY E., *tug*	Stranded at Au Sable	1906
PILOT, *schr*	Collision near Caseville in Saginaw Bay and stranded	1896
PILOT, *tug*	Burned on Moon River, Georgian Bay	1910
PIONEER, *schr*	Foundered 10 miles off Duck Island	1871
PLATT, JAS., *schr*	Foundered in Straits, salvaged (sank elsewhere)	1874
PLOUGHBOY, *stmr*	Burned in Georgian Bay as T.F. PARKS	1870
PORT HURON, CITY OF, *stmr*	Foundered off Lexington	1876
PORTLAND, *schr*	Stranded at False Presque Isle, total wreck	1867
PORTSMOUTH, *prop*	Foundered and burned on Middle Island Reef	1867

NAME OF SHIP	AREA OF LOSS	DATE
POTTER, H.C., schr	Lost in northeast gale in Lake Huron	1891
PRAIRIE STATE, bge	Lost at Sand Beach	1879
PRAIRIE STATE, stmr	Lost in Straits	1860
PRESTO, schr	Broke up and sank off Harbor Beach	1895
PRICE, CHAS., stmr	Foundered near Port Huron, 28 lost in "BIG" storm	1913
PRINCE OF WALES, schr	Lost near Detour	1835
PRINCE, stmr	Foundered in Lake Huron, swamped by storm winds	1905
PRINDIVILLE, prop	Stranded and broke up near Oscoda	1882
PRINGLE, MARY, prop	Burned off Port Huron	1893
PRINGLE, WM. H., tug	Burned off Port Huron	1877
PROVOST, schr	Lost in Lake Huron	1887
PULASKI, schr	Ashore and wrecked at Grosse Pte north of Mackinac Island	1887
QUEBEC, stmr	Foundered on Magnetic Reefs at Cockburn Island, later raised, salvaged and then re-sank 1885 in St. Mary's River	1878
QUEEN CITY, bge	Lost in Lake Huron (1,000 ton steamer made into barge, Pte aux Barques)	1863
QUEEN CITY, schr	Lost on Hog Island Reef	1895
QUIXOTE, DON, stmr	Lost in Lake Huron	1836
RAAB, LUCY, schr	Foundered near Middle Island Reef	1862
RACER, brig	Stranded in Hammond Bay, total loss	1869
RACINE, schr	Pte aux Barques Reef	1892
RALEIGH, schr	Lost at Portage Bay, Manitoulin	1869

NAME OF SHIP	AREA OF LOSS	DATE
RANDALL, DORCAS, schr	Burned at Harbor Beach	1914
RATHBURNE, E.W. schr	Lost off Goderich in Lake Huron, crew saved	1886
RAYNOR, ANNIE C., schr	Stranded on Middle Island Reef	1863
RAYNOR, WM., schr	Foundered off Lexington	1883
READ, W.P., stm-bge	Foundered off Alpena in Thunder Bay	1917
REBECCA, schr	Sank off Detour, raised and re-sank near Alabaster	1872
REDFERN, prop	Foundered in Tawas Bay, off the point	1930
RED BOTTOM, schr	Foundered on Middle Island Reef	1876
REED, FRANK, tug	Wrecked near Barrie Island, North Channel	1899
REEVES, KITTY, schr	Lost in Saginaw Bay by Tawas Point (copper ship)	1870
REGINA, stmr	Foundered off Harbor Beach, "Big" storm victim	1913
REGINA, schr	Lost off Cove Island, Georgian Bay	1881
REID, JAMES, prop	Foundered near Byng Inlet in Georgian Bay	1917
REID, KATE, tug	Burned on the river in Saginaw	1873
REINDEER, bge	Foundered near 40 Mile Point in northeast gale, total loss	1895
REINDEER, schr	Sank at dock at Port Huron	18--
RELIEF, tug	Burned on the Saginaw River	1867
REMORA, prop	Foundered in the Straits, burned at St. Ignace	1892
REPUBLIC, prop	Lost in Lake Huron, ashore near Alpena	1898
REVELRY, slp ycht	Sank off Rogers City	1975

REPUBLIC...Steamer of 2,316 g.t., built in Cleveland in 1890...stranded in Lake Huron in 1898.

NAME OF SHIP	AREA OF LOSS	DATE
REYNOLDS, GEO. E., stmr	Burned in the Saginaw River at Bay City	1872
RHODES, schr	Lost in Lake Huron	1905
RICE, JOHN, schr	Foundered off Thunder Bay Island	1893
RICH, A.J., schr	Wrecked near Kincardine	1864
RICHMOND, C.Y., tug	Lost on Lake Huron	1868
RICHMOND, KATE, schr	Sank north of Lexington	1885
RIPPLE, ycht	Wrecked west of Lyal Island Light	1905
RIVERSIDE, schr	Wrecked on Garden Island Reef	1887
ROANOKE, schr	Lost near Alpena in Thunder Bay	1866
ROANOKE, stmr	Burned off 14 Mile Point	1894

NAME OF SHIP	AREA OF LOSS	DATE
ROBERTS, E.K., prop	Burned at Cook's Dock in Bayfield Sound under the name MICHIPICOTEN	1927
ROBERT, K., tug	Burned at Tobermory in Georgian Bay	1935
ROBERTSON, MARY R.	Burned at Byng Inlet, Georgian Bay	1878
ROCK QUEEN, stmr	Sank 10 miles north of Port Sanilac	1856
ROCKAWAY, schr	Lost in Lake Huron off Goderich	1858
ROCKET, schr	Collision 10 miles north of Pte aux Barques	1860
ROEN, MARQUIS, stmr	Burned on the river in Bay City	1932
ROSE, schr	Lost in Georgian Bay	1851
ROSEDALE, stmr	Wrecked on Charity Island in Saginaw Bay	1897
ROUNDS, W.H., schr	Stranded at Black River Reef, Thunder Bay in the "Big" storm	1905
RUELLE, GRACE, stmr	Lost near Port Austin, Saginaw Bay	1899
RUMBALL, JENNIE, schr	Foundered in Lake Huron near Goderich	1882
RURAL, schr	Stranded near Caseville in Saginaw Bay	1873
RUSSELL, schr	Sank in collision, St. Mary's River, 3 lives lost	1882
RUSSEL ROQUE, tug	Burned at Gore Bay	1931
RUSSIA, stmr	Sank near Detour, valuable cargo lost	1909
RYAN, stmr	Total loss in heavy gale, Thunder Bay Island	1890
RYAN, CHAS., prop	Foundered off Sand Beach, Harbor Beach	1875
SACRAMENTO, stmr	Foundered on Port Austin Reef in Saginaw Bay	1917

NAME OF SHIP	AREA OF LOSS	DATE
SAGAMORE, tug	Foundered off Harbor Beach	1936
SAGINAW, bge	Burned near Port Huron (converted from a steamer in 1869)	1905
SALINA, stmr	Sunk by LIZZIE A. DAW near Bay City	1895
SALVOR, stmr	Foundered off Manitoulin in Georgian Bay	1917
SAMSON, bge	Burned and lost on Lake Huron	1879
SANDUSKY, brig	Lost at the Straits, 7 lives lost	1856
SANDUSKY, CITY OF, stmr	Foundered in Lake Huron	1895
SANTIAGO, schr	Lost near Pte aux Barques	1918
SARONIC, stmr	Burned on Cockburn Island	1916
SATURN, stmr	Foundered north of Southhampton	1901
SAUCY JIM, tug	Burned by Christian Island, Georgian Bay	1910
SAWYER, J.D., schr	Stranded and broke up on Seul Choix Point	1893
SAWYER, W.H., stmr	Foundered near Harbor Beach Lighthouse	1929
SAYMO, tug	Lost near Club Island in Georgian Bay	1935
SCHOOLCRAFT, stmr	Burned at Midland, Ontario	1920
SCOTT, ISAAC, stmr	Foundered near Port Elgin, 28 lives lost, "BIG" storm	1913
SCOTT, THOS. R., stmr	Lost off Cabot's Head in Georgian Bay	1914
SCOVILLE, DAVID, tug	Burned at Sarnia	1879
SCOVILLE, PHILO, schr	Wrecked near Tobermory	1889
SEA GULL, bge	Burned at the Tawas docks (built in 1864 as a schooner sailed to Africa in '66 as a brig, made bge same year)	1888

SAGINAW...*Freighter of 508 g.t., built in Marine City in 1866...burned near Port Huron in 1905.*

L.C. SMITH...*Freighter aground and foundered at Nine Mile Point... 1905*

NAME OF SHIP	AREA OF LOSS	DATE
SEA GULL, tug	Burned in the Straits off Bois Blanc Island	1893
SEA GULL, tug	Sank in Saginaw Bay after collision off Linwood	1889
SEA GULL, prop	Burned at Tawas in Saginaw Bay	1890
SEA HORSE, schr	Stranded at Fitzwilliam Island in Georgian Bay	1871
SEA QUEEN, tug	Burned at Meldrum Bay	1932
SEARCHLIGHT, tug	Foundered near Harbor Beach	1908
SEATON, L., schr	Lost near Pte aux Barques, Saginaw Bay, totaled	1892
SECRET, prop	Burned at Star Shoal in Georgian Bay	1871
SEYMOUR, R.A., stmr	Sank at Port Washington	1889
SEYMOUR, WM., stmr	Foundered near Lonely Island in Georgian Bay	1877
SEVERN, schr	Wrecked at Cove Island	1895
SHAMROCK, stmr	Foundered near Alpena, Thunder Bay in "BIG" blow	1905
SHANDON, schr	Lost in Wingfield Basin, Georgian Bay	1884
SHANNON, schr	Foundered in Georgian Bay	1870
SHAW, JOHN, schr	Lost near Au Sable Point, Saginaw Bay	1894
SHAW, J.E., schr	Foundered off St. Helena Island	1856
SHELDON, THOS. P., schr	Collision northeast of AuSable Point	1901
SHEPHERD II, tug	Wrecked on reef at Lyal Island	1980
SHERIDAN, bge	Lost north of Lexington	1866
SHERWOOD, NELLIE, schr	Foundered in Georgian Bay at Cabot Head, all lost	1882
SHICKLUNA, prop	Foundered near Algoma Mills, North Channel	1883

NAME OF SHIP	AREA OF LOSS	DATE
SHUPE, WM., schr	Foundered near Port Huron, 4 lives lost	1894
SIBERIA, stmr	Foundered in Lake Huron (year of "BIG" blow)	1905
SIGNAL, stmr	Burned at Midland, Georgian Bay	1905
SILVERSPRAY, stmr	Burned at Owen Sound	1877
SIMONS, WILLIAM, bge	Burned off Thunder Bay Island	1933
SIMCOE, stmr	Sank between Providence Bay and Duck Islands	1880
SINGAPORE, schr	Lost near Kincardine Harbor	1904
SIMCOE, stmr	Sank between Providence Bay-Duck Islands, 16 lost	1880
SMITH, ANNA, stmr	Foundered near Cheboygan, 1 life lost	1889
SMITH, ELLA, tug	Sank in French River on Georgian Bay	1895
SMITH, H.P., tug	Burned in Saginaw River	1872
SMITH, J.A., schr	Lost at the Straits of Mackinac near Station Point	1887
SMITH, L.C., stmr	Foundered near Nine Mile Point	1905
SMITH, SOPHIA, bge	Lost in Lake Huron	1874
SMOKE, KITTIE, tug	Burned at the mouth of Saginaw River	1889
SNOW DROP, schr	Totaled on North Point, near Thunder Bay Island	1892
SON & HEIR, schr	Foundered in Georgian Bay, total loss	1869
SOPHIA, schr	Lost in Georgian Bay	1854
SOUTHWESTERN, schr	Lost in collision off Pte aux Barques	1850
SPANGLER, K., schr	Foundered off Presque Isle	1860
SPAULDING, J.M., schr	Stranded above Fort Gratiot	1905
SPAULDING, M.B., schr	Burned off Forester	1860

ST. MARIES...Propeller 1,357 g.t., built in Detroit in 1883 as a steam ferry...lost in Lake Huron south of Sturgeon Point in 1888.

NAME OF SHIP	AREA OF LOSS	DATE
SPORT, *tug*	Foundered off Lexington	1920
SPRY, ELLEN, *schr*	Total loss in gale near Shillagalee/Straits	1887
ST. ANDREW, *schr*	Stranded ashore near Cheboygan after Peshtigo collision	1878
ST. ANTHONY, *schr*	Lost near Goderich	1856
ST. CATHERINES, CITY OF, *stmr*	Foundered off Sand Beach	1880
ST. CLAIR, *schr*	Foundered at Pte aux Barques Reef, Saginaw Bay	1855
ST. CLAIR, *barge*	Sank at Harbor Beach, 5 lives lost	1888
ST. JOSEPH, *tug*	Foundered near Chantry Island	1875
ST. MARIES, *stmr*	Lost south of Sturgeon Point	1888
STALKER, M., *schr*	Collision near Cheboygan with the WAUGASHENE	1886

NAME OF SHIP	AREA OF LOSS	DATE
STANLEY, scow	Foundered in Georgian Bay	1859
STAR, schr	Sank in Georgian Bay with 6 lives lost	1852
STAR, tug	Burned in the Saginaw River at Saginaw	1869
STARLIGHT, schr	Burned in Georgian Bay, 4 lives lost	1883
STEELE, GEO., schr	Ashore and stranded near Oscoda	1898
STEVENS, O., bark	Lost in Georgian Bay, wrecked	1867
STEVENS, J.H., schr	Burned at Presque Isle	1927
STEVENS, W.H., schr	Stranded on Scarecrow Reef, Thunder Bay	1863
STOCKMAN, H.D., schr	Lost in Saginaw Bay, built at Au Sable	1894
STORM SPIRIT, schr	Collision in Lake Huron	1864
STRANGER, schr	Stranded near Caseville, Saginaw Bay	1873
STREET, CHAS. A., stmr	Burned near Richmondville	1908
STRONG, ELIZA, stmr	Burned on Lake Huron near Lexington	1904
SULTAN, schr	Sank near Port Hope	1873

* *In the late 1930's when high winds swept the water out of the Saginaw River, the hull of the SAMUEL STEPHENSON was discovered near the Third Street bridge in Bay City, Michigan.*

SULTANA, schr	Foundered in Lake Huron	1863
SUMMIT, schr	Stranded off Tawas Point, Saginaw Bay	1872
SUNRISE, bark	Lost in Lake Huron near Bois Blanc Island	1871
SUPERIOR, bge	Wrecked at Oak Point, Saginaw Bay	1895
SUPERIOR, stmr	Burned near Detour	1928
SUPPLY, schr	Lost in Lake Huron	1832
SURPRISE, tug	Burned in Georgian Bay	1905

NAME OF SHIP	AREA OF LOSS	DATE
SWAN, tug	Burned in Saginaw River in East Saginaw	1875
SWEETHEART, schr	Foundered above Port Huron	1880
SWEEPSTAKES, schr	Sank in the Big Tub, Georgian Bay	1896
SYRACUSE, schr	Sank off 40 Mile Point	1863
TABLE ROCK, bge	Foundered off Tawas Point, Saginaw Bay	1872
TARRYNOT, schr	Lost at Bois Blanc Island	1860
TAWAS, tug	Boiler explosion near Sand Beach and Port Huron	1874
TAWAS, CITY OF, bark	Lost in lake storm	1877
TAYLOR, HELEN, stmr bge	Foundered by St. Helena in the Straits	1923
TECUMSEH, bge	Lost near Port Huron	1881
TECUMSEH, stmr	Burned at Goderich	1909

SWEETHEART...Schooner of unknown origin...foundered in Lake Huron above Port Huron in 1880.

NAME OF SHIP	AREA OF LOSS	DATE
TELEGRAM, stmr	Burned by Fitzwilliam Island, Georgian Bay	1908
TEMPEST II, stmr	Burned in Parry Sound, Georgian Bay	1909
THEW, W.P., stmr	Lost in Thunder Bay, Lake Huron in a collision	1909
THOMPSON, EMMA E., stmr	Burned at Enola Island in the Georgian	1914
THOMPSON, MAGGIE, schr	Sank at Port Huron	1871
THORNTON, schr	Foundered southeast of False Detour after collision	1870
THOUSAND ISLANDER, stmr	Sank near Thunder Bay	1928
TIFFANY, J.H., schr	Collided with MILWAUKEE in Straits, 5 lives lost	1859
TIGER, tug	Burned in Bay City on Saginaw River	1870
TILDEN, S.J., schr	Lost near Port Huron following collision	1886
TODMAN, N.H., schr	Foundered on Lake Huron	1881
TOLEDO, tug	Lost on river in Bay City	1880
TOLEDO, stmr	Wrecked in Straits area	1869
TOPAZ, VII, ycht	Burned near Rogers City	1941
TOPSY, schr	Ashore on St. Martin's Pt. (later salvaged)	1891
TORRENT, JOHN, tug	Burned at Richards Landing	1913
TORRENT, IDA M., schr	Burned in Straits near Cross Village	1893
TORRENT, NELLIE, stmr	Burned on St. Mary's River	1899
TOWNSEND, OSCAR, prop	Burned off Port Sanilac	1891
TRADER, prop	Explosion on Lake Huron, 3 lives lost	1866
TRAFFIC, stmr	Total wreck near Sebewaing, Saginaw Bay	1868
TRAFFIC, tug	Burned in Saginaw	1869
TRANSLAKE #3	Capsized in Georgian Bay	1958

NAME OF SHIP	AREA OF LOSS	DATE
TREMBLE, M.E., schr	Lost in collision near Port Huron	1890
TREAT, WM., schr	Foundered off Port Albert	1883
TROY, stmr	Foundered in Saginaw Bay, 23 lost	1860
TROY, stmr	Boiler explosion, 1850, 22 lives lost, later wrecked at Goderich	1860
TRUANT, tug	Burned at Burnt Island, Manitoulin	1894
TURNER, ALVIN, stmr	Burned on the Georgian	1905
TURRET CROWN, stmr	Stranded near Meldrum, Britomart Points, (released)	1924
TWILIGHT, bark	Lost off Port Sanilac, 7 lives lost	1871
TYPO, schr	Collision near Presque Isle, 9 lives lost	1899
UGANDA, stmr	Sank near White Shoals	1913
UNCLE SAM, tug	Crushed in the ice in the Straits and sank	1882
UNION, tug	Burned in Saginaw Bay	1870
UNION, stmr	Burned at Port Huron	1867
UNITED STATES, stmr	Burned at Sarnia	1927
VALENTINE, schr	Lost on Port Austin Reef in Saginaw Bay	1873
VANDERBILT, schr	Burned near Serpent Island, Georgian Bay	1882
VAN VALKENBERG, LUCINDA, schr	Collision north of Thunder Bay Island	1887
VENICE, CITY OF, stmr	Sank in a Saginaw Bay collision	1902
VENUS, schr	Sank in Thunder Bay with all hands lost	1887
VERBENA, MAY, tug	Lost in Lake Huron, wrecked in Stokes Bay	1896

UNITED STATES...Passenger steamer—burned at dock in Sarnia in 1927.

NAME OF SHIP	AREA OF LOSS	DATE
VERMILION, stmr	Burned in Lake Huron, 5 lives lost (raised, rebuilt as NEW ORLEANS)	1842
VIATOR, stmr	Collision off Thunder Bay	1935
VICTOR, schr	Foundered in Lake Huron, south of Sand Beach with total loss	1888
VICTORIA, prop	Lost in Lake Huron near Kettle Point	1884
VICTORIA, tug	Foundered in Georgian Bay	1896
VICTOIRE, MARIE, schr	Lost in Saginaw Bay	1887
VIENNA, schr	Foundered north of Thunder Bay Island	1906
VITA, ycht	Lost off Yeo Island in Georgian Bay	1910
VOLUNTEER, schr	Foundered on Port Austin Reef, Saginaw Bay	1893
VOLUNTEER, schr	Wrecked and sank in big storm	1869

NAME OF SHIP	AREA OF LOSS	DATE
WABASH, stmr	Sank in collision off Lexington (hit Empire State)	1870
WALKER, C.H., schr	Lost in Lake Huron	1876
WALTERS, JOHN, schr	Foundered near Russell Island, Georgian Bay	1899
WALRUS, schr	Lost on Gray's Reef in the Straits	1868
WANDERER, schr	Sank at Kincardine	1883
WARD, EBER, stmr	Foundered at Straits of Mackinac, 5 lives lost	1909
WARD, J.P., stmr	Burned in Saginaw River at Bay City and rebuilt	1865
WARD, MARY, stmr	Lost near Collingwood on Nottawasaga Shoal	1872
WARD, SUSAN, bge	Lost in storm near Oscoda	1885
WARREN, WM. C., stmr	Stranded off Presque Isle	1947
WARNER, CHAS. M., stmr	Lost near Nine Mile Point	1905
WARNER, JOHN F., schr	Lost in Lake Huron near Alpena	1890
WARRINGTON, H., stmr	Wrecked in heavy lake storm	1869
WATER WITCH, prop	Lost in Saginaw Bay with 28 lives lost	1863
WATERLOO, stmr	Wrecked on Georgian Bay	1846
WATT, ANNIE, stmr	Collision on Lake Huron	1890
WATTS, J.G.	Foundered on Devils Island Shoal, Georgian Bay	1895
WATSON, MARY, stmr	Wrecked in storm between Kincardine and Goderich	1858
WAUBUNO, stmr	Wreckage and capsized hull found near Moose Pt. 30 lives lost (some estimates as high as 70 lost)	1879
WAURECAN, bge	Foundered at Port Austin Reef, Saginaw Bay	1875
WAUSEDA II, tug	Burned at Fitzwilliam Island, Georgian Bay	1948

NAME OF SHIP	AREA OF LOSS	DATE
WAVE, schr	Lost in Lake Huron, 2 lives lost off Inverhuron	1858
WAVE, stmr	Burned at Charity Island, Saginaw Bay	1874
WAVERLY, stmr	Collision off Harbor Beach	1903
WAVETREE, schr	Lost in Lake Huron	1868
WAWINET, tug	Lost south of Beausoleil Island, Georgian Bay	1942
WAYNE, schr	Stranded at Au Sable Point, Saginaw Bay	1875
WEAVER, NETTIE, schr	Total loss in wreck near Kincardine	1877
WEEKS, CHAS. H., schr	Foundered near Port Huron, 1 life lost	1889
WELCOME, slp	Lost in Straits storm, all hands	1787
WELLINGTON, schr	Wrecked at Skillagalee	1867
WELLS, JARVIS, schr	Wrecked at Sand Beach, Lake Huron	1879
WESLEY, JOHN, schr	Lost at Pte aux Barques, Saginaw Bay	1894
WESTERN STAR, schr	Wrecked near Goderich and sank	1854
WESTERN STAR, stmr	Wrecked on Clapperton Island, North Channel	1915
WESTFORD, stmr	Burned in Georgian Bay at John's Island	1904
WESTOVER, stmr	Burned at Au Gres River	1881
WETMORE, W.L., stmr	Wrecked on Russell Island, Georgian Bay	1901
WEXFORD, stmr	Foundered near Kettle Pt., all hands lost in "BIG" storm	1913
WHITAKER, BYRON, stmr	Lost in Lake Huron, burned to the waterline	1920
WHITE FOAM, schr	Sank off Bois Blanc Island in the Straits	1899
WHITE, KIRK, schr	Foundered in Saginaw Bay	1869

NAME OF SHIP	AREA OF LOSS	DATE
WHITE SQUALL, schr	Collision in Saginaw Bay, 7 lives lost	1872
WHITE STAR, stmr	Burned at Cheboygan	1844
WHITE SWAN, tug	Wrecked at Skillagalee, Straits area	1959
WILCOX, O., tug	Foundered off Tawas Point, sank in 7 minutes	1893
WILLIAMS, A.B., schr	Lost in Lake Huron storm	1864
WILLIAMS, C.P., brig	Foundered near Port Austin, Saginaw Bay	1886
WILSON, BELLE, stmr	Foundered in Thunder Bay	1888
WILSON, D.M., prop	Foundered northeast of Thunder Bay Island	1894
WIMAN, schr	Lost on Pte aux Barques Reef	1855
WINDSLOW, stmr-bge	Burned at Meldrum Bay	1910
WINDSOR, ELIJAH, stmr	Foundered near Port Huron	1901
WINNANA, prop	Burned at Tobermory, Georgian Bay, mailboat	1909
WINNIPEG, CITY OF, stmr	Burned in Georgian Bay	1881
WINONA, S.S., stmr	Burned at Spragge	1929
WINSLOW, KATE, schr	Sank at Meldrum Bay (salvaged and lost later in 1897 in Lake Michigan)	1881
WINSLOW, ANNIE, brig	Wrecked at Duck Island	1852
WINSLOW, R.G., bark	Wrecked at Spectacle Reef	1867
WINSLOW, RICHARD, schr	Lost at the Straits of Mackinac, White Shoals	1898
WITCH, tug	Sank in Saginaw Bay	1869
WITCH OF THE WEST, tug	Burned in Saginaw Bay off river mouth	1904
WOLF, LOTTIE, schr	Wrecked, north shore of Hope Island, now a reef	1879
WORTHINGTON, GEO., schr	Foundered near St. Helena - saved	1875
WOLSEY, GENERAL, stmr	Burned on Georgian Bay near Cape Croker	1886

YUKON...Schooner of 1,602 g.t., built in 1893 in West Bay City,... lost in Lake Huron squall in 1905.

NAME OF SHIP	AREA OF LOSS	DATE
WOODRUFF, J.S., schr	Wrecked on Georgian Bay	1886
WOOLSON, MARY, stmr	Lost with tow barge at Sturgeon Point	1920
WYOMING, bge	Lost near Port Huron	1876
WYOMING, stmr	Foundered near Port Austin in Saginaw Bay	1904
YANKEE, schr	Lost near Port Elgin	1893
YANKEE BLADE, schr	Lost near Skillagalee...saved to sail again	1883
YORK STATE, schr	Foundered in Georgian Bay	1886
YOUNG, ANNIE, prop	Burned near Lexington with 9 lives lost, 13 saved by EDWARD SMITH	1890
YOUNG LYON, schr	Burned in Lake Huron	1874
YOUNG, WM. A., schr	Foundered south of Middle Island	1911

NAME OF SHIP	AREA OF LOSS	DATE
YUKON, *schr*	Lost in Lake Huron	1905
ZEALAND, *stmr*	Disappeared on upper Lake Huron (former CHATHAM)	1880
ZENITH CITY, *stmr*	Foundered in Hammond Bay	1916

Postscript to the Adventure

In tracking these shipwrecks of Lake Huron we stumbled onto a number of interesting and intriguing sets of circumstances often resulting in a coincidence. It happened more often than not. We also encountered a few research frustrations along the way, and dotted our final "i" and crossed our last "t" with a few interesting conclusions.

One prime source for much of the information contained in this book was Mansfield's "HISTORY OF THE GREAT LAKES", published by Beers of Chicago in 1899. In this comprehensive cataloguing of wrecks, frequently we would find a vessel sunk as the result of a collision but seldom would the involved second vessel be indentified. Later, as we proceeded to sift through the hundreds upon hundreds of shipwrecks listed in this work, as well as in dozens of reference works, we'd run across a vessel that had also been sunk by collision in the same area, as well as the same year, as had been shown by our first example. While our listings did not always indicate that these two vessels had collided with each other, it did provide a fascinating and viable possibility. You might find it intriguing to see how many "collision" listings you can match up by area and date.

One annoying and frustrating situation was frequently encountered when our research would find a listing that would read, "WHITE, JONATHON, schooner, burned Lake Huron, 1878". Such a listing opened a "pandora's box" of possibilities relative to the exact location of disaster. It could have occurred anywhere on Lake Huron; it might conceivably have happened on Saginaw Bay inasmuch as this body of water *is* a part of Lake Huron; the same could be said for Georgian Bay and North Channel or the Thunder Bay-Presque Isle waters. In other words, we found ourselves in a position where it was impossible to place these wrecks in specific locations. None of our research material proved helpful in these instances. As a result of this lack of location information our totals for our separate sections can only reflect those wrecks that we *definitely* tracked to those areas.

We were amazed by the number of vessels which "disappeared" in a given year. A number of them show up in the old records, and the disaster that befell these vessels, regardless of its nature or form, could have happened anywhere on the Great Lakes. Or on the St. Lawrence and the Atlantic for that matter. History has simply recorded these ships as being with us one year and gone the next. In the past few years as we've pored over these records, checking and re-checking our findings time after time, we believe it is safe to say that there are almost as many unidentified listings for Lake Huron as there are definitive descriptions of the locale of collisions, wrecks, fires and sinkings that we have assembled and compiled for this book.

One conclusion that any researcher on a project of this magnitude and nature has to reach, is that the Great Lakes have a voracious appetite for ships and sailors. The fact that so many of the ships disappeared in the 18th and 19th centuries has to be attributed to the total lack of communications. When a ship left a port in those days its skipper and crew were totally "on their own." Plus, there were hardly any navigational aids prior to the 20th century and so you have all the necessary ingredients for a sea-going disaster. If a skipper and his ship failed to show up at a designated destination, and if the shipping season ended without any word of him or his vessel, they were considered as "lost". The vessel went into the record books for that year as having "disappeared"...the locale of its demise was unknown.

As pointed out earlier in this book, Lake Huron's shipwrecks have *not* been published before in an organized, alphabetized form. Nor have they all (or as many as we could locate) been presented before in their own book, within the framework of their own being. The disaster statistics for Lake Huron have been scattered at random through better than 50 books, pamphlets and marine reference manuscripts making it virtually impossible for anyone, including freshwater historians, to grasp the enormity of all that has transpired here since man began keeping records.

We remind you once again, "SHIPWRECKS OF LAKE HURON...the Great Sweetwater Sea", is *not* an official inventory of shipwrecks. It is, instead, the end-result of a hobby grown tall in the doing. When we found that our record-seeking and sorting showed Saginaw Bay contained 187 shipwrecks, as opposed to an earlier historically supported published figure of 24, we allowed our enthusiam to take us on a track through all the waters of Lake Huron. We sincerely hope you have found it as interesting in the reading as we did in the five years we invested in our research, checking, sorting and seeking the truth.

We could do it no other way!

ACKNOWLEDGEMENTS:

This book, and the research it entailed, would have been impossible without the help, encouragement and unselfish cooperation of a number of wonderfully understanding people.

Ralph Roberts of Saginaw, Michigan, who supplied all our historical photographs from his personal and private collection, was also most generous with his efforts of help, encouragement, counsel, advice and direction in both our search and subsequent research.

Cathy Baker, Great Lakes Historian of Essexville, Michigan was most generous with all her material, as she has always been. Work that she did on her "Ship Building on the Saginaw", while concerned with construction, did, of necessity encounter and entail much that dealt with the ultimate disposition of these vessels. This voluminous record was ours to work with, thanks to Mrs. Baker.

Les Arndt, longtime editorial writer and columnist for the Bay City Times and author of several books of regional history, contributed much through his columns, books and letters.

Kenneth Teysen of Mackinaw City, Michigan drew us deep into the legend and lore of the Straits area with his fascinating Mackinaw Museum, and Ken was always available to answer a question and offer a clue.

Harvey Peltz, Stan Lenz and Leonard Flewelly, of Rogers City, gave us much to consider and include, Harvey calling on his lifetime at WLC, Rogers City; Stan from his years on the docks at the city marina; and Leonard from the First Mate's position on the bridge of the CALCITE.

Ivan Trick of Meldrum Bay, Jack McQuarrie, of Gore Bay, and Byron "Barney" Turner of Little Current, all on Manitoulin Island were all of great help with detail and data relative to the North Channel.

Dr. Charles Feltner, of Dearborn, Michigan, one of the leading authorities on wrecks in the Straits area, gave invaluable assistance in checking and solidifying findings in this section of the work.

Art O'Hara, Business Manager of the Great Lakes Historical Society, in Vermilion, Ohio was an unexpected, unselfish and wholly sincere guide through the entire maze of Great Lakes wrecks. We can also say that without Art's friendly, generous and interested assistance and never-ending help, starting with day number one and continuing to the present, this would have been a *far different* and less cohesive work than you now have in hand.

A number of previous authors and researchers, as noted in the bibliography, were also of inestimable value to the total project.

We must here also acknowledge the encouragement and assistance that was accorded us by our friends and fellow members of the Great Lakes Cruising Club. Interest displayed by their Chicago office personnel, as well as their assistance, made the endless work all worthwhile.

Finally, my wife Beth, who has cruised the Great Lakes with me for a lifetime and who was not only unselfishly patient and understanding throughout the project but a vital factor in its eventual completion as well, deserves a standing ovation! Her faith never faltered as endless months turned into years over musty old records, books, papers, ship's logs, charts, wreck reports and other material as we checked and rechecked our findings. Additionally, she alphabetized all of our wreck lists and typed every word of the manuscript, as well as those lists, time after time after what had to seem "impossible" time!

To all of these, plus others who helped in a hundred ways, our deepest thanks and appreciation. Without their help we'd never have reached port!

Bibliography

ALCONA, THE LAKE PIONEERS .... Doris Gauthier
AMERICAN VOYAGEUR .... Douglas
BLUE WATER BOUNDARY .... Malkus
BY THESE WATERS .... Arndt
DIRECTORY OF SHIPWRECKS...................... Heden
DRUMMOND ISLAND .... Cook
EXPLORE WISCONSIN SHIPWRECKS ..... Kimm Stagelfeldt
FATE OF THE GRIFFON .... McLean
FREIGHTERS OF FORTUNE .... Beasley
GEORGIAN BAY, SIXTH GREAT LAKE .... Barry
GHOST SHIPS OF THE GREAT LAKES .... Boyer
GREAT LAKES .... Hatcher
GREAT LAKES COUNTRY .... McKee
GREAT LAKES PILOT, VOL. II .... U.S. Dept. of Commerce
GREAT LAKES SHIPWRECKS & SURVIVALS .... Ratigan
GREAT LAKES SHIPWRECKS .... Great Lakes Gazette
GREAT STORIES OF THE GREAT LAKES .... Boyer
GREAT LAKES STRANDINGS............... U.S. Coast Guard
HISTORY OF LES CHENEAUX ISLANDS............. Grover
HISTORY OF MELDRUM .... Wickett
HISTORY OF MICHIGAN'S THUMB .... Schultz
HISTORY OF THE GREAT LAKES .... Beers/Mansfield
INLAND SEAS.................. Great Lakes Historical Society
LAKE HURON .... Landon
LAKE HURON DIVE CHART ...... Midwest Explorer's League
LONG SHIPS PASSING .... Havighurst
MACKINAC ISLAND & SAULT STE MARIE .... Newton
MANITOULIN .... Major
MANITOULIN ECHOES .... Munroe
MARINE CASUALTIES OF GREAT LAKES
    .... U.S. Lifesaving Service
MEMORIES OF THE LAKES .... Bowen
MICHIGAN... Dunbar
NORTHERN MICHIGAN HANDBOOK FOR
    TRAVELERS....................................... Inglis
PASSING OF AN ERA .... Townsend
SHIPBUILDING ON THE SAGINAW .... Baker
SHIPS & MEN OF THE GREAT LAKES .... Boyer
SHIPWRECKS OF LAKE SUPERIOR .... Wolff
SHIPWRECKS OF THE LAKES...................... Bowen
SHIPWRECK REPORTS (District 8 & 10) ..... U.S. Coast Guard

STEAMER WRECKS 1831-1930 .... Captain Edward Carus
STRAITS OF MACKINAC .... Ratigan
THE NORMAC .... Townsend
THE SALVAGER, THE LIFE OF CAPTAIN TOM REID
   OF THE GREAT LAKES .... Doner
THE 1912 "SPECIAL" .... Gore Bay Recorder
THREE FLAGS AT THE STRAITS .... Havighurst
TRUE TALES OF THE GREAT LAKES .... Boyer
WENJIDA .... Gore Bay Recorder
WINDS OVER LAKE HURON .... Sinclair
WRECKS & CASUALTIES OF THE GREAT LAKES FROM
   1895, 1896 & 1897 .... U.S. Dept. of Agriculture
WRECKS WHICH OCCURRED ON THE GREAT LAKES FROM
   Dec. 17, 1885 - Nov. 15, 1893 .... U.S. Dept. of Agriculture
WRECK REPORT OF GREAT LAKES
   .... U.S. Dept. of Agriculture
YONDER OUR ISLAND .... McDonald

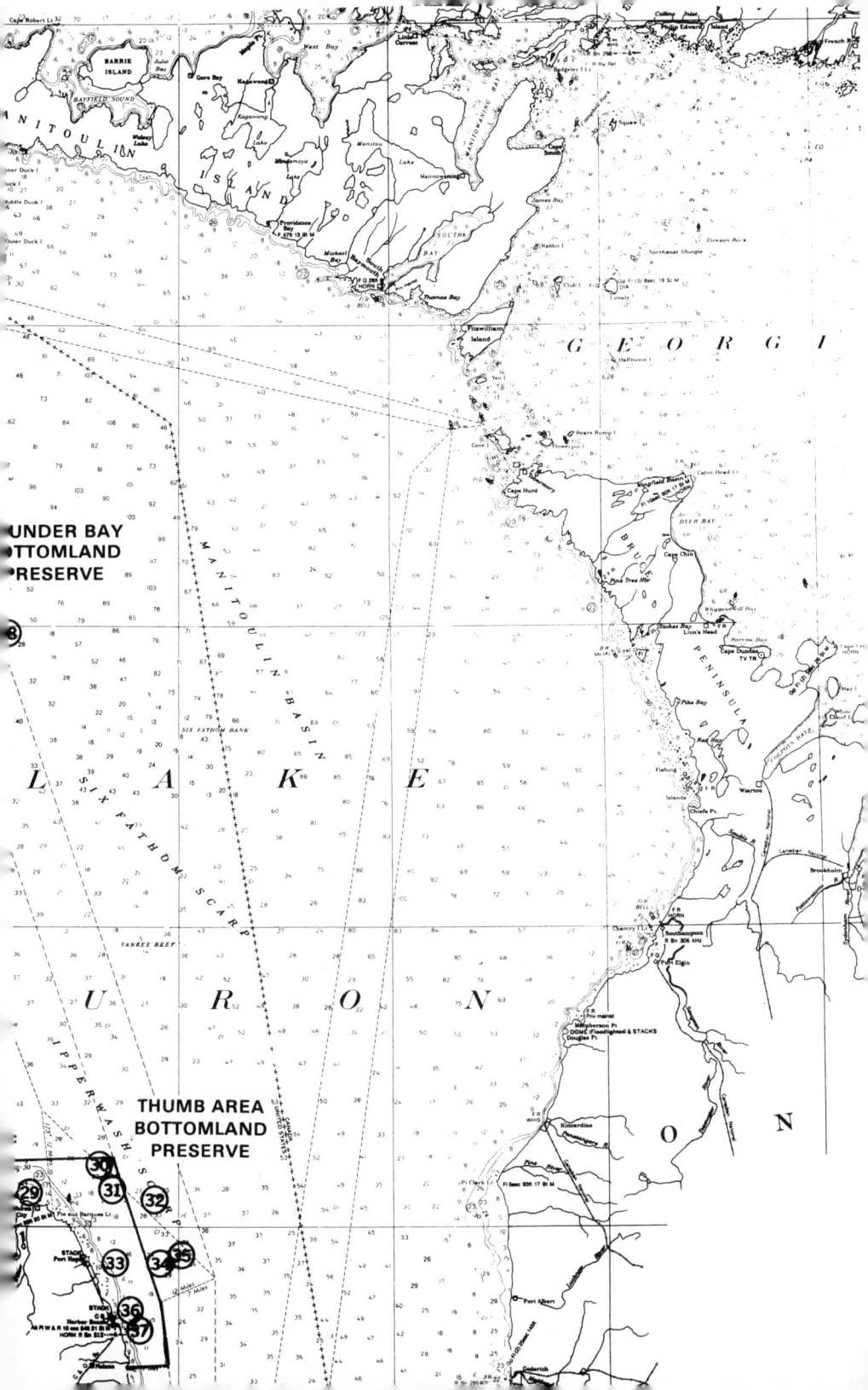

STRAITS OF MACKINAC BOTTOMLAND PRESERVE

(1) *MINNEAPOLIS:* Sunk by ice in Straits, broke up in dive to bottom. 4 m NE of McGulpin's Pt, 400′ W of bridge. Depth 124′.

EBER WARD: Cut by ice and foundered in 5 to 10 minutes. 270 deg, 4.35 m from S tower of Mackinac Bridge, on ledge on S side of Channel at 135′.

(2) *M. STALKER:* Sail vessel sunk in collision with Waubanshene near Cheboygan. ¾ m NW of Cedarville wreck, buoyed, Depth 90′.

(3) *CEDARVILLE:* Propeller cap 2 m E from Mackinaw beach after collision with steamer Topdalsfjord. Depth 110′.

(4) *W.H. BARNUM:* Steamer foundered 10 m SE of Mackinaw City. Intact and upright at 74′.

(5) *HENRY CLAY:* Wood centerboard sail vessel foundered 4 m NW of Cheboygan. Depth 65′.

(6) *NEWELL A. EDDY:* Sail vessel parted her towline and disappeared. Presumed to have been found between Bois Blanc I. and Spectacle Rf.

THUNDER BAY BOTTOMLAND PRESERVE

(7) *NEW ORLEANS:* Wood steamer collision with steamer Lynn, 9.2 m 354 deg from Thunder Bay I. Depth 148′.

(8) *NORDMEER:* German steel steamer aground on rocks of Thunder Bay Shoal off Alpena. Top of wreck above water, charted and buoyed. Depth 40′.

(9) *UNKNOWN:* Wood sail vessel 5 m 354 deg from Thunder Bay I LtHo. Charted and buoyed. Depth 35′.

(10) *ISAAC M. SCOTT:* Steamer last 7 m N of Gratiot LtHo found 7 m NE of Thunder Bay LtHo. Inverted at 175′.

(11) *UNKNOWN:* Wood sail vessel on E side of North Pt 1 m N of S tip. Depth 15′ to 20′.

(12) *ENTERPRISE:* British steamer stranded 1 m off Sta North Pt on reef, Thunder Bay.

UNKNOWN: Wood sail vessel ashore ¼ m NNE of S tip of North Point, depth 15′.

GALENA: Passenger steamer stranded North Pt Rf.

(13) *D.M. WILSON:* Wood steamer foundered 4.6 m 23 deg from Thunder Bay I. LtHo. Intact in 60′.

(14) *D.R. HANNA:* Steel steamer foundered after collision with Quincy A. Shaw 6 m 56 deg off Thunder Bay I Lt. Vessel inverted, 90′ off surface. Depth 140′.

(15) *JAMES DAVIDSON:* Wood steamer stranded and sank ½ m E of Thunder Bay Lt. Depth 45′.

MONOHANSETT: Wood propeller burned and sank ½ m W of Thunder Bay Lt. Depth 20′.

(16) *LUCINDA VAN WALKENBURGH:* Sail vessel foundered after collision 22 m 143 deg from Thunder Bay I Lt. Depth 105′.

(17) *VIATOR:* Norwegian steel steamer collided with Ormidale 8.9 m 112 deg from Thunder Bay I Lt. Depth bow 190′; stern 250′.

(18) *MONROVIA:* Liberian steel propeller collided with Can propeller Rozalton and foundered 107 deg, 13½ m from Thunder Bay I Lt. Depth 150′.

(19) *PEWABIC:* Wood steamer foundered after collision with steamer Meteor, 6.7 m 130 deg from Thunder Bay I Lt. Depth 165'. Intact and upright.
(20) *GRECIAN:* Steel steamer collided and foundered 5.1 m 176 deg from Thunder Bay I Lt. Vessel was raised but sank here on way to drydock. Depth 105'. Intact.
(21) *MONTANA:* Sidewheel steamer, burned and foundered 226 deg 5 m from Thunder Bay I Lt. Depth 70'.
(22) *J.T. JOHNSON:* Wood sch-barge, stranded on shoal 2 m W of S tip of North Pt. Depth 50'.
(23) *OSCAR T. FLINT:* Wood steamer burned and foundered 4½ m 120 deg from entrance Thunder Bay I. on shoal. Depth 33'.
(24) *UNKNOWN:* Wood steamer 1½ m E of entrance Thunder Bay R. Depth 24'.
(25) *MOLLY T. HORNER:* Wood sail vessel stranded on shoal 1 1/3 m NNE of South Pt. Depth 18'.
(26) *GOLD HUNTER:* Sail vessel ashore on Thunder Bay Rf on bar of Black R, 10 m N of Sturgeon Pt.

THUMB AREA BOTTOMLAND PRESERVE

(27) *EUGENE:* Sail vessel stranded on S side of Port Austin Rf.
S.H. KIMBALL: Sail vessel collided with towing steamer George Stone and foundered 3.8 m NW of Pt Aux Barques.
(28) *L. SEATON:* Sail vessel ashore 1½ m NNW of Point Aux Barques Sta.
KEYSTONE STATE: Sidewheel passenger steamer bound Detroit for Milwaukee, last seen 3 m NE off Port Austin. Wreckage foundered off Pt Aux Barques.
OSCEOLA: Steamer foundered 1½ m 35 deg off Port Austin.
(29) *BERLIN:* Sail vessel. Struck Burned Cabin Reef 1 m above Grindstone City.
ALBION: Can sail vessel barge stranded 1¼ m 56 deg from Grindstone City.
MAGGIE ASHTON: Steamer stranded 3½ m 80 deg off Grindstone City.
(30) *ALBANY:* Steel propeller collided with propeller Philadelphia, taken in tow, but Albany went down in 30 m about 8 miles NE of Pt Aux Barques Lt. Depth 148'.
(31) *PHILADELPHIA:* Steel propeller collided with propeller Albany, took Albany in tow. When she foundered, tried to make shore, but foundered 5½ m NE of Pt Aux Barques Lt. Upright and intact in 124'.
(32) *HUNTER SAVIDGE:* Sail vessel cap near Pt Aux Barques Lt. 10 m 45 deg off Port Hope.
(33) *E COHEN:* Sch-barge stranded 8¾ m 158 deg off Pt Aux Barques Lt on Port Hope Rf.
(34) *R.G. COBURN:* Passenger propeller foundered 6½ m off Harbor Beach. Intact in 21 fm.
(35) *MINNEDOSA:* Can 4 mast sail vessel, while under tow of steamer Westmount, foundered 8 m NE of Harbor Beach.
(36) *H.A. EMERY:* Sail vessel stranded 1⅛ m NNE of Harbor Beach Sta while attempting to enter hbr.
COL. BROCKETT: Sail vessel stranded 1 m NE of Harbor Beach Sta alongside of Breakwater.

CHICKAMAUGA: Double deck barge-sch, foundered 1 m N of Harbor Beach, was removed to 1 m outside of hbr. Depth 35'.

(37) *ST. CLAIR:* Sail vessel barge, foundered 1 1/3 m SE off Harbor Beach.

PESHTIGO: Wood steamer, stranded 1240' off LtHo, Harbor Beach.

GEO. H. WAND: Sail vessel stranded off Harbor Beach.

MICHIGAN GREAT LAKES BOTTOMLAND RESOURCES

Due to an increase in commercial and recreational diving in the Great Lakes, a serious threat to Michigan's underwater resources has been posed. In response to this problem, the Michigan Legislature adopted Public Act 284 of 1980 (amending Act 173 of P.A. 1929). The act provides for the designation of underwater preserves, for preservation of abandoned property on the bottomlands of the Great Lakes, and for the issuance of salvage permits where appropriate.

Act 184 is administered jointly by the Department of Natural Resources and the Department of State. The Department of Natural Resources reviews the recreational aspects of abandoned property while the Department of State reviews the historical significance. Although the statute is administered by the state, a burden of making the law effective clearly falls upon the diving population. The Great Lakes divers must also recognize the value of underwater resources and comply with this law to preserve these valuable resources.

DEFINITIONS FOR ACT 184, P.A. 1980

Abandoned Property

An aircraft or watercraft, and all equipment of the craft, and all personal property of the people of the craft, which have been deserted, relinquished or left behind and for which attempts at reclamation have been abandoned by owners or insurers. In addition, all materials resulting from activities of historic and prehistoric Indians.

Great Lakes Bottomlands

The unpatented lake bottomlands of Lakes Erie, Huron, Michigan, St. Clair and Superior.

Great Lakes Bottomlands Preserve

An area located on the bottomlands of the Great Lakes and extending upward to and including the surface of the water which is delineated by the Department of Natural Resources for special protection of abandoned property of historical value, or ecological, educational, geological, or scenic features of formations having recreational, educational, or scientific value. A preserve may encompass a single or a collection of several objects, features or formations. Great Lakes bottomlands preserves will be limited to not more than five percent of the Great Lakes bottomlands within Michigan.

Historical Value

Value relating to, or illustrative of, Michigan history, including the statehood, territorial, colonial, and historic and prehistoric Indian periods.

Recreational Value

Value relating to an activity which the public engages in, or may engage in, for recreation or sport, including scuba diving and fishing.

Michigan Great Lakes Underwater Resources

TO OBTAIN APPLICATION FORMS OR ADDITIONAL INFORMATION CONTACT:

Submerged Lands Unit
Division of Land Resource Programs
Department of Natural Resources
P.O. Box 30028
Lansing, Michigan 48909
517/373-1950

or

Museum Section
Michigan History Division
Department of State
528 N. Capitol Avenue
Lansing, Michigan 48918
517/373-0515

*Michigan Great Lakes
Underwater Resources*

Special thanks to Jim Hein, Michigan Department of Natural Resources, Marquette, for his help and information.

Additional information can be obtained from:

The Straits of Mackinaw Great Lakes State Bottomland Preserve
Mr. Bill Becks
1157 Hinkley Blvd.
Alpena, Michigan 49707

Thumb Area Bottomland Preserve
Huron County Parks
417 S. Hawselmaw
Bad Axe, Michigan 48413
517/269-6404
Steven P. Romzek

Thunder Bay Bottomland Preserve
Linda Bedell
517/356-1736

Alpena Area Chamber of Commerce
P.O. Box 65
Alpena, Michigan 49707
517/354-4181

GLOSSARY

prop—propeller, steamship driven forward with rotating propeller blades.

schr—schooner, any of various types of sailing vessels having a foremast and mainmast, with or without other masts, and having fore-and-aft sails on all lower masts.

stmr—steamer, vessel propelled or operated by steam.

bark—barkentine or bark, vessels having three or more masts, square-rigged. Vary in which masts are square-rigged.

tug—tugboat, a small, powerful boat for towing or pushing ships, barges, etc.

*scow—*any of various vessels having a flat-bottomed rectangular hull with sloping ends, built in various sizes with or without means of propulsion, as barges, punts, rowboats, sailboats, etc.

*brig—brig or brigantine,*two-masted vessel, square-rigged on both masts.

*stm. bge—steam barge,*steam powered barge

slp—sloop, a single-masted, fore-and-aft-rigged sailing vessel, with or without a bowsprit, having a jib-headed or gaff mainsail, the latter sometimes with a gaff topsail, and one or more headsails.

bge—barge, a flat-bottomed vessel, usually intended to be pushed or towed for transporting freight or passengers; lighter.

ycht—yacht, a vessel used for private cruising, racing or other noncommercial purposes.

dredge—a barge in which powerful machines capable of removing earth from the bottom of a river are mounted.

gunboat—a small vessel carrying mounted guns—capable of moving in shallow waters.

mv—motor vessel

g.t.—gross tonage

We at Avery Color Studios thank you for purchasing this book. We hope it has provided many hours of enjoyable reading.

Learn more about Michigan and the Great Lakes area through a broad range of titles that cover mining and logging days, early Indians and their legends, Great Lakes shipwrecks, Cully Gage's Northwoods Readers (full of laughter and occasional sadness), and full-color pictorials of days gone by and the natural beauty of this land. Beautiful note stationery is also available.

For a free catalog, please call 800-722-9925 in Michigan or 906/226-3338, or tear out this page and mail it to us. Please tape or staple the card and put a stamp on it.

PLEASE RETURN TO:

P.O. Box 308
Marquette MI 49855

CALL TOLL FREE
1-800-722-9925

Your complete shipping address:

_____
_____
_____

_____

Fold, Staple, Affix Stamp and Mail

_____
_____
_____

Avery COLOR STUDIOS

P.O. Box 308
Marquette MI 49855